Artificial Intelligence and the Future of Healthcare

The application of Artificial Intelligence (AI) in the healthcare sector is certain to boost levels of automation and productivity but, paradoxically, it will also increase the availability of "first line competence." At the same time as demographic trends are affecting demand for health and social care, the technological developments we are seeing make it highly likely that AI will play a decisive role in tackling the challenges our healthcare systems will encounter. This book reveals systemic connections to tackle questions about the potential impact of AI on future challenges in the healthcare sector.

Specifically, it develops practical proposals for ways in which AI can be applied to solve these forthcoming issues. It emphasizes the importance of AI in what is known in the literature as human augmentation. The book's innovative perspective is apparent in the way it challenges conventional wisdom in the context of several pressing questions, such as:

- What opportunities and challenges could arise from the application of AI in the healthcare sector?
- How can the philosophy of medicine, viewed from a systemic perspective, help us to understand, explain, and resolve some of the future challenges in the healthcare sector?
- How could AI affect inclusive employment opportunities for people with disabilities?

The book also contains an underlying argument to the effect that the rational approach adopted by economists is perhaps less rational when applied to a healthcare sector that is crying out for more "first line competence."

The primary readership will be academic, but the book will also appeal to policymakers, consultants, HR departments, healthcare stakeholders, and related practitioners.

Jon-Arild Johannessen is Full Professor of Leadership at Kristiania University College, Norway.

Routledge International Studies in Health Economics

Edited by **Charles Normand**, Trinity College Dublin, Ireland and **Richard M. Scheffler**, School of Public Health, University of California, Berkeley, USA

Reconfiguring Global Health Innovation
Padmashree Gehl Sampath

Public Policy and the Public Interest
Lok Sang Ho

Economics and HIV
The Sickness of Economics
Deborah Johnston

Medical Innovation
Science, Technology and Practice
Edited by Davide Consoli, Andrea Mina, Richard R. Nelson and Ronnie Ramlogan

Politics, Hierarchy, and Public Health
Voting Patterns in the 2016 US Presidential Election
Deborah Wallace and Rodrick Wallace

Equity and Healthcare Reform in Developing Economies
The Case of Turkey
Songül Çınaroğlu

The Digital Transformation of Healthcare
Health 4.0
Edited by Marek Ćwiklicki, Mariusz Duplaga and Jacek Klich

Social Finance and Health
Neil McHugh, Olga Biosca and Cam Donaldson

Artificial Intelligence and the Future of Healthcare
Jon-Arild Johannessen

Artificial Intelligence and the Future of Healthcare

Jon-Arild Johannessen

Routledge
Taylor & Francis Group
LONDON AND NEW YORK

First published 2025
by Routledge
4 Park Square, Milton Park, Abingdon, Oxon OX14 4RN

and by Routledge
605 Third Avenue, New York, NY 10158

Routledge is an imprint of the Taylor & Francis Group, an informa business

British Library Cataloguing-in-Publication Data
A catalogue record for this book is available from the British Library

Library of Congress Cataloging-in-Publication Data
Names: Johannessen, Jon-Arild, author.
Title: Artificial intelligence and the future of healthcare/Jon-Arild Johannessen.
Description: Abingdon, Oxon; New York, NY: Routledge, 2024. |
Series: Routledge international studies in health economics |
Includes bibliographical references and index.
Identifiers: LCCN 2024015718 (print) | LCCN 2024015719 (ebook) |
ISBN 9781032803685 (hardback) | ISBN 9781032805368 (paperback) |
ISBN 9781003497325 (ebook)
Subjects: LCSH: Artificial intelligence–Medical applications. |
Artificial intelligence–Economic aspects. | Medical economics.
Classification: LCC R859.7.A78 J64 2024 (print) | LCC R859.7.A78 (ebook) |
DDC 610.285/63–dc23/eng20240416
LC record available at https://lccn.loc.gov/2024015718
LC ebook record available at https://lccn.loc.gov/2024015719

ISBN: 978-1-032-80368-5 (hbk)
ISBN: 978-1-032-80536-8 (pbk)
ISBN: 978-1-003-49732-5 (ebk)

DOI: 10.4324/9781003497325

Typeset in Times New Roman
by Deanta Global Publishing Services, Chennai, India

Contents

Figures

Preface

In this book, we explore problems relating to artificial intelligence (AI) and future challenges in the healthcare sector. Our general question can be framed as follows: What is the potential impact of AI on future challenges in the healthcare sector? To tackle this general question, we have chosen to explore the following sub-questions:

- How can AI contribute to increasing the numbers of "first line competence" in the healthcare sector?
- What opportunities and challenges could arise from the application of AI in the healthcare sector?
- How can the philosophy of medicine, viewed from a systemic perspective, help us to understand, explain, and resolve some of the future challenges in the healthcare sector?
- How could AI affect inclusive employment opportunities for people with disabilities?

Many current trends suggest that future challenges in the healthcare sector will pose a major problem for even the wealthiest societies. Demographic trends will affect healthcare systems in many countries, including Western countries, China, and elsewhere. The large numbers of people who will live into their seventies, eighties, and beyond can be seen as a kind of ticking time bomb for healthcare systems around the world. Population ageing will make it essential to modify, or even completely overhaul, health and social care systems, in order to provide sufficient care for the growing numbers of older people.

At the same time as demographic trends are affecting demand for health and social care, the technological developments we are seeing make it highly likely that AI will play a decisive role in tackling the challenges our healthcare systems will encounter.

Core message

The application of AI in the healthcare sector will boost levels of automation. But paradoxically, AI will also increase the availability of "first line competence."

Statement of aims

What is this book about?
In this book, we aim to provide descriptions, examples, analyses, and theoretical reflections. In addition, we attempt to show the real-life benefits of various aspects of our theoretical reflections by providing practical examples. We also reveal systemic connections, in order to tackle questions about the potential impact of AI on future challenges in the healthcare sector.

Specifically, our aim is to develop practical proposals for ways in which AI can be applied to solve future challenges in the healthcare sector.

What are the main themes and objectives?
We know that demographic trends in most countries will exacerbate challenges in the healthcare sector. We can also be relatively certain that AI will boost productivity in healthcare systems, as well as elsewhere in society. The extent to which this productivity increase will be reflected in greater numbers of "first line competence" in the healthcare sector, or alternatively in cost-cutting exercises, is a political rather than a technological question.

The models that all of us use, in order to understand and explain social phenomena lead to the formation of mindsets, which in turn trigger actions. In this book, we emphasize that the opposite can occur: actions can change mindsets. We believe that we can use actions to change our attitudes and mental models.

In this book, we emphasize the importance of AI in what is known in the literature as human augmentation. Possibly, the biggest revolution for people with disabilities in the innovation economy and the Fourth Industrial Revolution will be precisely this: human augmentation.

What are you doing differently, in a more innovative way, or better than existing books?
Our book differs from other books on the healthcare-related challenges associated with demographic trends and technological progress because we take a positive view of the potential of new technologies, for example in increasing numbers of "first line competence." In addition, we stress that AI-related boosts in productivity will increase the need for "first line competence," in order to address emotional and social challenges at all levels in the healthcare sector.

Our book's innovative perspective is apparent in our focus on workplace inclusion for people with disabilities. According to conventional wisdom, AI and other new technologies will exacerbate the problems faced by people with disabilities. In our view, however, AI will facilitate the inclusion of people with disabilities in the workplaces of the future.

The book also contains an underlying argument to the effect that the rational approach adopted by economists is perhaps less rational when applied to a healthcare sector that is crying out for more "first line competence." Accordingly, we are proponents of the following hypothesis: The greater the involvement of economists in healthcare systems, the less the capacity for emotional and social perspectives.

Part I

Artificial intelligence in healthcare

1 Future health challenges

Core idea

The application of AI in the healthcare sector will boost levels of automation. But paradoxically, AI will also increase the availability of "first line competence."

Key points

- Demographic trends are exacerbating crises in healthcare systems.
- Stagflation may exacerbate healthcare challenges.
- Future healthcare challenges will be negatively impacted by US–China "decoupling."
- Increasingly hostile relations between the United States and China have the potential to exacerbate healthcare challenges.
- The more AI becomes integrated into our healthcare systems at various levels, the greater the need to integrate social and emotional intelligence into leadership systems at the same levels.
- We can propose the following hypothesis: The greater the involvement of economists in healthcare systems, the less the capacity for emotional and social perspectives.
- Healthcare challenges are coinciding with the climate, environmental, and inequality crises.

Introduction

The problems that we investigate in this book concern artificial intelligence (AI) and health-related challenges that will arise in the future. The current trends suggest that in the future healthcare challenges will pose major problems, even for the world's most affluent societies. In Western countries, in China, and elsewhere, demographic time bombs will necessitate the reassessment, modification, and restructuring of parts of – or even entire – healthcare systems. At the same time, technological progress will make it very likely that AI will play a decisive role in tackling future challenges in our healthcare systems. The use of intelligent automation could have at least two results: Either a major reduction or else a major increase in "first line competence" in the healthcare sector. As in other

DOI: 10.4324/9781003497325-2

sectors, perhaps the most likely outcome will be a kind of balance between intelligent automation and an increase in "first line competence." The outcome will depend, however, on our treatment of the many people who will relocate or flee from unsafe parts of the world due to climate crisis, environmental crisis, and armed conflict. In other words, we are experiencing a new industrial revolution based on AI and other technologies, while at the same time we are in the midst of at least three systemically linked crises.

Migration can have negative impacts on both the host and origin countries. The challenges can be many, but one of these challenges is related to access to medical services and the increased pressure on healthcare systems.

The demographic development in industrialized countries is such that a rapidly ageing population indicates that there are fewer working-age people, leading to a shortage of labour (Acemoglu et al., 2011; Roy, 2022). However, this problem may be addressed by increased migration. But for the origin countries, migration can have a negative impact due to loss of young and able-bodied people of working age. From a global perspective, the demographic development is a challenge for healthcare systems.

Population ageing also results in a decline in government revenue because fewer people pay income tax. At the same time, an ageing population puts significant pressure on government spending owing to rising healthcare costs. These challenges are particularly evident in Japan which not only has the highest proportion of elderly people in the world, but also a declining birth rate. The health challenges in Japan will increase in the future towards 2040–2050, because there will be fewer people of working age who can support the ageing population. In practice, the shortage of labour due to population ageing will most probably result in a reduction in pensions. In turn, this may result in a collapse of expectations and a situation where people no longer look forward to retirement, as was the case in the past.

With such a demographic development, the governments in Japan and Europe will have problems with the current tax systems, regarding the challenges related to maintaining pension levels and providing adequate healthcare for an ageing population (Roy, 2022). The financial pressure on government budgets will be challenged and creak at the joints, even if one redefines much of the funding of healthcare and pension systems. Many countries in Europe, as well as certain other countries and regions, with relatively good welfare benefits, may find themselves in a situation where pension schemes and healthcare are grossly underfunded (Roy, 2022). As mentioned above, this underfunding will be due to the reduction in the labour force, which will result in a decline in government revenue, because fewer people will be paying income tax. The underfunding can be solved in the short term by an increase in borrowing. In the slightly longer term, however, this is not a solution, but quite the opposite. A growing debt crisis can damage an economy more than the relief provided by borrowing to solve short-term challenges.

If future economic development in industrialized countries begins to resemble the developments we have seen in Japan, then stagflation and economic challenges could become an even greater challenge for healthcare systems than the demographic crisis. If, in addition to stagnant economic growth, inflation increases at the same time, as well as an increased decoupling of the United States and China, then the challenges facing the Western world may be very difficult to solve, especially in relation to what is the focus of this book: Future healthcare challenges.

In this book, we will address the following general question: What will the future challenges of artificial intelligence be in healthcare? To tackle this general question, we have chosen to explore the following sub-questions:

RQ1: How can AI contribute to increasing the numbers of "first line competence" in the healthcare sector?
RQ2: What opportunities and challenges could arise from the application of AI in the healthcare sector?
RQ3: How can the philosophy of medicine, viewed from a systemic perspective, help us to understand, explain, and resolve some of the future challenges in the healthcare sector?
RQ4: How could AI affect inclusive employment opportunities for people with disabilities?

In this book, we aim to provide descriptions, examples, analyses, and theoretical reflections. In addition, we attempt to show the real-life benefits of various aspects of our theoretical reflections by providing practical examples. The first three research questions are examined and answered in Part I of the book. The fourth research question is examined and answered in Part II of the book.

In the following, we make some introductory remarks related to the abovementioned research questions. Each of the research questions will be given a thorough examination in the respective chapters of the book where these questions will be examined.

How can AI contribute to increasing the numbers of "first line competence" in the healthcare sector?

The increased application of artificial intelligence (AI) within the healthcare industry has the potential for greatly increasing automation processes. The question that arises in this context is whether this will lead to a decrease in human input, i.e., a decrease in the so-called "first line competence" (frontline workers).[1] However, it is conceivable that the opposite effect will occur, namely that increased automation will lead to greater productivity and value creation, which can then be used to employ more "first line competence" in the healthcare sector. This is a political question and not merely a matter of unregulated technological development. Do we wish to have more frontline healthcare workers, or do we wish to streamline the healthcare sector and increase productivity? In other words, whether or not increased automation will result in fewer or more "first line competence" in the healthcare sector is not a technological problem that needs to be solved, but instead a political problem. Politicians say that we need to prioritize when resources are scarce. This is of course correct; however, how should you prioritize and for whom should you prioritize. It will of course be more costly to have more "first line competence" in the healthcare sector than if these "first line competence" were automated away by new technology. If it becomes a central public and political aim to increase the number of healthcare workers, rather than the opposite, then this will require increased governmental expenditure. One way of solving this problem when resources are scarce would be to restructure the taxation system. For instance, what if taxation levels in the Western world could be set to the level they were at around the beginning of the 1980s. If this measure were implemented, then most challenges in the healthcare sector and other areas of social welfare would most probably be solved. There is no historical evidence that indicates that the taxation systems of the early 1980s led to an economic crisis – neither for the wealthy, nor the average taxpayers. If this tax reform was introduced, the wealthy would have to pay considerably more in tax, while average taxpayers would pay more or less the same as they pay today. This could boost the number of "first line competence" in the healthcare sector as well as increase the number of frontline workers in other public welfare sectors, by bringing the tax system in the Western world back to the level of the early 1980s.

What opportunities and challenges could arise from the application of AI in the healthcare sector?

New technology can be used for good and bad purposes, i.e., it can be a boon or a bane for society. In the case of artificial technology (AI) it is how we choose to utilize new technology that determines if we help or harm ourselves and others. In other words, we need to use AI in a planned and more optimal way. If we do this, it can benefit our lives. The possible negative consequence of the future development of AI technology is that humans may lose control of its development. If this happens, the technology could do more harm than good. This fear has been expressed by key figures such as Stephen Hawking and other scientists who signed an open letter describing the possible dangers associated with the unfettered future development of AI technology.[2]

AI-driven sectors, not directly related to the healthcare sector, may also affect the need for medical care. For instance, the development and increased use of self-driving cars could greatly decrease accident injuries, leading to less strain on the healthcare system. In other words, many such technological innovations, based on artificial intelligence, will be able to reduce the pressure on the healthcare sector. This possibility cannot be ignored, even though Hawking and the other signatories of the open letter mentioned above make an important point that if this technology gets out of control, we will then face major challenges in many areas.

Artificial intelligence (AI) is being used to improve medical treatments and increase productivity in healthcare. AI is also being used in other sectors to automate work tasks and increase productivity, such as the transport and energy sectors. In other words, the new technology is being used in several sectors to automate work tasks. Using technology to automate work tasks and increase productivity has been happening steadily since the First Industrial Revolution and has gained pace throughout the last two centuries. From a short-term perspective, such a development has been a direct threat to workplaces. For instance, prior to the First Industrial Revolution, most weaving was done by domestic workers. However, the introduction of weaving machines resulted in domestic weavers losing their jobs. This created a volatile situation. The weavers banded together and became known as the "Luddite weavers." They carried out militant actions raiding new textile factories and destroying the weaving machines. However, from the long-term perspective, more new jobs were created, productivity increased, and there was a general rise in wages and prosperity. But this was a slow process, so it is doubtful that this long-term development benefitted the Luddite workers who had lost their jobs.

Since the First Industrial Revolution, significant advances have been made in medical knowledge, resulting in greatly improved healthcare.[3]

Today, there are few people who have extensive knowledge of artificial intelligence and how it has gradually developed from the first steps that were made around the 1950s, when cyberneticists conducted their first experiments. Moreover, few people know what the social consequences of the further development of artificial intelligence will be. However, we know that future AI applications will most probably have a great potential for helping people with complex illnesses.

In this chapter, we will suggest the following proposition: The more that AI becomes integrated into our healthcare systems at various levels, the greater the need will be to integrate social and emotional intelligence into leadership systems at the same levels.

Throughout the centuries, humans have continually developed their knowledge. However, it is only in the last 250 years that technology has made vast advances. Since the 1950s, and especially from around the 2000s, artificial intelligence (AI) and robotics have been developing at record speed. Against this background, it might be assumed that at some point in the future AI will surpass human intelligence, and be able to design the architecture of future healthcare systems. It has already been shown that chess computer programs can beat world chess champions. Taking into consideration the future development of AI, AI programmes will then most probably be able to develop the design architecture of future healthcare systems.

However, one thing is certain regarding how artificial intelligence will be able to re-design our hospitals and our healthcare systems, and this is that a major focus will be upon value. This value can be measured in relation to various parameters, such as perceived satisfaction regarding medical treatment. Some theorists might say that the most important indicator of value in healthcare is "the health outcome per dollar of cost expended" (Porter & Teisberg, 2006). It is possible that Porter and Teisberg have an important point related to economic factors when scarce resources are the focus of analysis. However, it is also worth reflecting on the fact that redesigning healthcare systems will probably also involve a redefinition of our values and perspectives related to those people who will need future healthcare services. It is not certain that it is appropriate to use parameters that can be "counted, weighed and measured" in any context related to future healthcare challenges. From such a perspective, it will possibly be the social and emotional competencies that become important at an overall level, in order to solve the healthcare challenges of the future, and not simple economic determinism. In this context, one can propose the following hypothesis: The greater the involvement of economists in healthcare systems, the less the capacity for emotional and social perspectives.

In the same way that artificial intelligence continues to transform our societies on most levels, it is possible to imagine that this technology can also transform how we think in relation to those who are in need of our healthcare systems. The economic logic need not in any way be the only, or even the foremost way of thinking, to solve problems related to scarce resources. During the Age of Reason people began to think differently. The new focus was on rigorous scientific discourse, with less focus on mysticism and obscure thinking, which was often shown to be irrational. Similarly, the future "Age of AI" will probably change the way we think. When AI chess machines can find winning chess moves that no chess champion had ever seen before, and when AI can be used to discover new antibiotics that scientists have been unable to create, then it is not improbable that AI will change our way of thinking, so that there will be less focus on rational economic models, and more focus on models based more on social and emotional intelligence. If this occurs, then it is highly probable that we will be able to redefine the healthcare sector according to new perspectives.

How can the philosophy of medicine, viewed from a systemic perspective, help us to understand, explain, and resolve some of the future challenges in the healthcare sector?

Many topics that are discussed within the field of healthcare are comprehensive, and based on assumptions about central factors that are under development. Some of these factors are related to demographic developments, especially in Western countries, but also in China. Other assumptions are related to how the new technology is being developed and what future opportunities may result in considerable consequences. These topics are also related to philosophical reflections regarding medical expertise, although it is no easy matter to draw clear distinctions here (Bunge, 2013). Regarding these reflections, the ethical perspective related to the development of new technology is important. For instance, should one use new technology and health resources to keep very old people alive, i.e., people between 90 and 100, and older? In other words, the development of new health technology will also involve discussing the various ethical aspects. These ethical discussions need not necessarily be directly related to medical expertise, although the question of what expertise is available will provide factual input for discussions.

The new AI technology can be helpful in making the right medical diagnosis. For example, AI algorithms can analyse medical images, such as X-rays, CT scans, and so on, and assist medical personnel in identifying and diagnosing diseases accurately and quickly. Artificial intelligence will also be able to ensure tailored treatments and better quality of treatments. Another future application of AI is to gain a better understanding of placebo response. For example, such an application could investigate the unwanted side effects of a placebo.

If new AI technology can improve medical treatments, then the increased use of AI medicine will also result in the necessity of discussing various ethical issues in relation to new treatments. It is also conceivable that new AI technology will be used to develop healthcare management systems, optimize workflows, and improve efficiency.

How could AI affect inclusive employment opportunities for people with disabilities?

The first global report on "disability" was published by the World Health Organization in 2011. This report determined that approximately 1 billion people could be classified as "disabled people." In 2016, 150 countries signed the UN Convention on the Rights of Persons with Disabilities (CRPD) (Slorac, 2016: 9). The rights of people with disabilities have probably never been better than they are today. In contrast, we also know that people with disabilities find it difficult to enter the labour market (Austin, 2019). We can often read in the newspapers about personal tragedies concerning soldiers who have been injured or wounded in war, and who, on returning home, can't find jobs (Driedger, 1989). On the other hand, we can also read stories about people with multiple disabilities who, despite all the challenges they meet, are still able to succeed. For example, Helen Keller, who became the first deaf and blind person to gain a BA degree; and who later became an advocate for the rights of people with disabilities.[4]

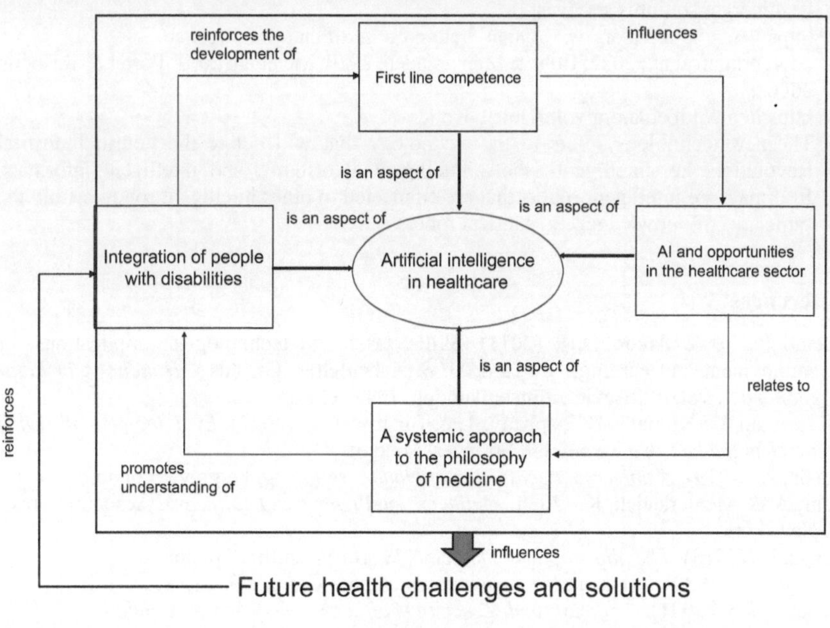

Figure 1.1 Artificial intelligence in the healthcare sector: A conceptual model.

What is meant by "disability"? "Disability" can be defined as a physical, mental, cognitive, or developmental impairment that reduces or limits a person's ability to carry out certain tasks or participate in activities and interactions. Many disabilities are not necessarily visible to others. There are various degrees and types of disability. Various terms are used when speaking about people with disabilities, such as dysfunction, impairment, disablement, handicap, incapacity, infirmity, special needs, and so on. The use of such terms is often linked to various models and concepts related to disability. The way people use terms, concepts, and models can often affect people's behaviour, for example towards people with disabilities. This also relates to how organizations relate to this group of people in terms of employment. Important, in this context, is the extent to which new technology will introduce new perspectives regarding the employment of people with disabilities. It is precisely the question regarding the future development of artificial intelligence and the needs of people with disabilities in relation to entering the labour market that we will elaborate on in Part II of this book.[5]

Figure 1.1 provides a figurative summary of the general research question and the four research questions reviewed above. Figure 1.1 also shows the way this book is structured.

Notes

1 "First line competence" is a metaphor used in the healthcare services in Scandinavia for good care and nursing, also in relation to the importance of possessing adequate professional skills and knowledge. Roughly translated, this refers to health professionals who work in the frontline and who deal directly with patients, clients, or other users of a health organization's services.
2 https://en.wikipedia.org/wiki/Open_Letter_on_Artificial_Intelligence
3 AL-Turmjan et al.; 2022; Bohr & Memarzadeh, 2020; Mahajan, 2021; Porter & Teisberg, 2006.
4 https://en.wikipedia.org/wiki/Helen_Keller
5 The new technology refers to the technology that will define the Fourth Industrial Revolution, i.e. intelligent robots, intelligent algorithms, and intelligent informats. Informats are intelligent robots that are connected to other intelligent robots within the same area of knowledge, e.g. surgical robots.

References

Acemoglu, D. & Autor, D.H. (2011). Skills, tasks and technologies: Implications for employment and earnings, in Card, D. & Ashenfelter, O. (eds.), *Handbook of labor economics*, vol. 4, Elsevier, Amsterdam, pp. 1043–1171.

Al-Turmjan, F.; Kumar, M.; Staphany, T. & Bhardwaj, A. (2022). *Evolving role of AI and IoMT in the health care market*, Springer, London.

Austin, A. (2019). *A universal declaration of human wellbeing*, Palgrave, London.

Bohr, A. & Memarzadeh, K. (2020). *Artificial intelligence in healthcare*, Academic Press, New York.

Bunge, M. (2013). *The philosophy of medicine*, World Scientific, London.

Driedger, D. (1989). *The last civil rights movement*, St. Martin's Press, New York.

Mahajan, P.S. (2021). *Artificial intelligence in healthcare*, MedMantra, London.

Porter, M.E. & Teisberg, E.O. (2006). *Redefining health care: Creating value-based competition on results*, Harvard Business School Press, Boston.

Roy, A. (2022). *Demographics unravelled: How demographics affects and influence every aspect of economics, finance and policy*, Wiley, New York.

Slorac, R. (2016). *A very capitalist condition, A history and politics of disability*, Bookmarks Publications, London.

2 First line competence

Core idea

In this chapter, technological developments are viewed from a dynamic perspective, and artificial intelligence (AI) is not viewed either positively or negatively.

Key points

- A growing number of specialist hospitals will implement robotic technologies. Meanwhile, smaller local hospitals will rely increasingly on AI.
- New organizational and leadership structures will focus on frontline services, i.e., services where there is direct contact between health professionals and service users, and where emotional and social competence are of crucial importance.
- AI will lead to explosive increases in productivity and the rate of automation of the entire healthcare sector.
- Mandatory service models will be developed with the objective of delivering services to individual users as locally as possible.
- As healthcare services are reformed, in order to increase their proximity to users, we can envisage the emergence of a new healthcare profession: Community therapists.
- It is possible to imagine healthcare stations being designed in accordance with the concept of 15-minute cities. Primary care services could be provided to users at healthcare stations, where they can be treated by health personnel with basic competence. Such healthcare stations could satisfy a significant need in local communities, and alleviate pressure in other parts of the healthcare system.
- Higher productivity will increase the availability of "first line competence" in various parts, and at various levels, of the healthcare sector.

Introduction

The challenges of future healthcare can be viewed in many different ways. One challenge concerns the level of demand for "first line competence" in the healthcare sector, i.e., for workers who can care for people who are unable to care for

DOI: 10.4324/9781003497325-3

themselves for reasons including sickness, age, and disability (Britnell, 2019: 160). One challenge faced by the healthcare sector is population ageing – an increase in the proportion of elderly people in the population (and a corresponding decrease in the proportion of young people). The resulting demographic imbalance will lead to a problematic increase in demand for workers in the healthcare sector. The general topic of this book is the impact of AI on future healthcare challenges, including the challenge of recruiting more carers. The general question addressed in this chapter is as follows: How can AI contribute to increasing the number of "first line competence" and improve users' experience of the healthcare sector?

This chapter utilizes a straightforward logic, which is that artificial intelligence will increase the automation of work tasks and replace jobs in most sectors; however, in the healthcare sector the automation of work tasks, and increased productivity, using new technology such as AI and robotics, will result in more frontline care providers being available, the so-called "first line competence." Many critics have suggested that an ageing population will result in a shortage of health professionals. However, we propose here that this may not necessarily be the case (Mahajan, 2021; Al-Turmjan et al., 2022). On the other hand, it will take time (time-lag) before the implementation of new technology results in increased automation and productivity. It is during this time lag that the healthcare sector may face challenges. But from a slightly longer perspective, any shortage of healthcare professionals will probably be solved, because of the automation of work processes and increased productivity, resulting in more frontline care providers being available.

As mentioned above, the application of new technologies will result in increased automation and productivity. Initially, this will mainly concern repetitive work tasks. Most probably, work tasks related to knowledge development, diagnosis, analysis, and surgical interventions, will also be supported or replaced by AI and robotics applications. The digitalization of healthcare will improve services and result in many organizational changes. However, this digitalization has also had negative effects initially, but this is often the case with the introduction of new technology. On the other hand, it has been shown throughout technological history that such initial problems are eventually solved (Frey, 2019; 2020).

Digitalization will also lead to reduced face-to-face communication, such as in the case of treatment, examinations, and so on (Bohr & Memarzadeh, 2020).

If the assumptions we have argued for above are shown to be true, that automation will lead to more, not fewer, "first line competence," and that digitalization processes will increase in the healthcare sector, then there will most probably be an increased focus on primary healthcare. This is in the frontline services where patients meet their doctor, nurse, midwife, and so on. If we also assume that new technology, such as AI and robotics applications, is also utilized in the primary healthcare services, then there is much to suggest that this will enable care to be shifted closer to home and thus ease pressure on hospitals. One can envision that smaller local hospitals will become the cornerstones of primary healthcare services. This can also be related to Carlos Moreno's[1] concept of the 15-minute city,[2] i.e., services being within a 15-minute walk of where people live. At these local hospitals, it will be possible to utilize AI and robotics applications, in order to increase the quality of services and treatments.

For the sake of the argument, let's examine how this will affect the larger hospitals. One can imagine that such a model will promote both quality and performance in the primary healthcare services. This will increase the status of employees, and probably lead to more people working in the local hospitals. For the larger hospitals, this can lead to specialization, where the new technology, such as AI and robotics, is extensively used. Robotic applications could be specially designed for various disease groups, such as cardiovascular ailments, cancer treatment, kidney surgery, eye surgery, and so on. With such a model, the larger hospitals will become specialized technology hospitals, while the smaller local hospitals will be able to deal with most of the lighter tasks.

The new organization of robotic hospitals, as well as high-tech local hospitals in the primary healthcare services, will also promote new forms of management. These new forms of management will very likely be oriented towards the development of quality and performance in the frontline, i.e., close to the patient or user. This implies that the new leaders will mainly need to have social and emotional skills, rather than skills in economic management, if they are going to be able to function well in the new organizational model. The financial management can be mainly organized at the departmental level. The point here is that financial management focuses mainly on the economic aspects of running a hospital, but not so much on the social aspects. If such a change in the management systems were to become a reality, then this would increase the likelihood of a stronger link between the management level, the frontline level, and the patient and user levels, in healthcare systems.

The challenge in the future for healthcare, in the transitional period where new technology is being implemented to improve productivity, will be to ensure that there is enough "first line competence." The importance of accomplishing this task is literally a matter of life and death, especially when there is a considerable lack of resources. In practice, this means that political measures need to be urgently implemented to deal with the shortage of healthcare providers which is predicted to increase in the future, as demand will outpace supply. When a war threatens, all our resources have to be used to resist an aggressor. It is this attitude that must be incorporated at the policy level, in order to be able to cope with the growing crisis we see in healthcare systems around the world. When a cat hunts a mouse, it is only a meal for the cat, while it is a matter of life and death for the mouse. It is the mouse's perspective that we have to focus on, not the cat's attempt to get a meal. The strategy that must be implemented by the political system can be called an urgency-strategy.

When artificial intelligence is fully implemented in the healthcare industry, as well as in the general economic system, it is most probable that the lack of "first line competence," i.e., healthcare workers, will cease to be a problem. The explanation is that increased automation will ease staffing shortages. However, the period before artificial intelligence is fully implemented may be characterized by a crisis in the industry. This is not unlike what we see occurring in the transition to the green economy. When the green economy has become a reality, many of the problems such as environmental risks, global warming, and ecological scarcity will largely be solved. However, during the transition to the green economy there will still be many problems. The same will most likely also happen in the healthcare sector in the period before the new technology has been able to take over many activities and processes. It is during this period that an urgency-strategy should be adopted; fighting the crisis may metaphorically be compared to fighting a war. In other words, urgent measures will have to be implemented, in order to address the shortage of healthcare workers.

The time gap between the implementation of AI and robotics in the healthcare industry, and the full transformation of the industry, will result in a temporary shortage of "first line competence" (frontline healthcare personnel). In this chapter, we view this challenge as one of the major problems that the healthcare industry will face in the future. It is during this time gap that an urgency-strategy should be adopted by the political authorities; in this context, fighting the crisis may be compared to fighting a war. In other words, the shortage of healthcare workers will literally be a matter of "life and death." The proposition we can formulate on the basis of the above description is fairly straightforward: The more "first line competence" we lack in our healthcare systems, the more likely it is that people will suffer and die needlessly, because help does not arrive in time. The proposition that can be formulated to solve this challenge is the following: The more we view the lack of "first line competence" in the healthcare sector as constituting a war-like situation against an aggressor, the greater the probability that we can solve this challenge.

As mentioned above, AI and robotics are on the brink of transforming the healthcare industry. In this context, apart from developing an urgency-strategy, the industry needs to start to prepare for these future changes. The reason for this is that it takes a long time to change norms, values, and attitudes. In other words, old norms and values can live on long after they have any real purpose. We have elaborated and exemplified this in Chapter 4, where we reflect on a systemic understanding of medical philosophy.

The idea is that the sooner we start changing organizational structure in the healthcare sector, the sooner we will have this new structure in place, to prepare for the situation when artificial intelligence and intelligent robots become fully operational. As mentioned above, the implementation of artificial intelligence and intelligent robots will increase automation and productivity (Britnell, 2019). However, this innovative technology will not necessarily change the way we organize and manage our healthcare systems (Frey, 2019). In other words, many of the major challenges we will face within healthcare will be largely related to the organization and management of the sector. It is against this background that the time gap that we referred to above should be used to tackle the challenges that are not solved as a result of new technology being introduced. It is in this context that the political system needs to make the right interventions. If this does not happen, we may risk having a situation where the technology solves many problems, but the consequences of the new technology create more challenges than necessary.

Narratives related to "first line competence"

Case letter 1: Health and 15-minute cities

Official reports in many countries describe skilled personnel as the backbone of the healthcare sector. Few people would disagree with this view. Opinions could change somewhat, however, if AI and intelligent robots become core technologies in most healthcare systems. Of course, no one knows exactly when this might happen. Kurtzweil (2005; 2008; 2013) proposes 2035–2045 as a realistic window for when new technologies could come to equal and surpass human intelligence. Regardless of when this happens and the extent to which AI becomes a crucial part of the healthcare sector, more "first line competence" are needed in all parts of the healthcare sector. In this connection, several commentators have noted that the healthcare and social care sectors must both be sustainable and also provide essential services close to where people actually live. It is in this context that we can begin to reflect on the urban-planning concept of the "15-minute city," which was proposed in 2021 by the urbanist Carlos Moreno.[3] According to Moreno, proximity to everyday necessities is crucial for a good quality of life. In a 15-minute city, all the most important everyday destinations, such as schools, shops, offices and other workplaces, healthcare, and leisure facilities, should be located within a short walk or cycle ride for the vast majority of residents. Another important consequence of proximity to these everyday facilities will be that dependence on cars for everyday travel will be reduced to a minimum. It is reasonable to assume, as do many of those who debate the concept of 15-minute cities, that this kind of strategy for urban development would tend to improve individuals' health and well-being.[4]

If one is to relate the future healthcare systems to the thinking around 15-minute cities, then it is imaginable that health systems will be redesigned at various levels. It is very possible that new designs at different levels of the healthcare system, and the functions that are shared between these levels, will promote this type of urban development. In order to achieve a situation where most people do not have more than a 15-minute cycle ride to their workplaces, this assumes that more remote working should be organized, or else hybrid working that combines remote work with in-person work. This organization of work emerged during the Covid-19 pandemic from 2020 to 2022, so it will not be difficult to integrate this way of working in the 15-minute city concept. This would also require urban development to be focused more on becoming pedestrianized and bike-friendly. In other words, less cars, more bicycles. In addition, there will be a need for more urban green spaces and play spaces for children. Moreover, in the future, healthcare systems and remote and hybrid working will require well-developed information and communication systems. In a practical context, this means that the focus on digitalization will be increased. The development of both 5G and 6G networks is gaining increasing importance in most areas. For the healthcare services, digitalization will be an absolute necessity. A simple reason for this is that the specialized hospitals will draw their cutting-edge competence from the global competence clusters. Artificial intelligence and intelligent robots, together with this cutting-edge expertise, would be able to perform medical interventions. They can only do this if the technological networks are optimized to cope with the necessary information exchange that is needed to carry out such tasks.

One does not need to imagine a vision of the future to find the basis for the concept of the 15-minute city. 15-minute cities have existed from antiquity to the medieval era. The cities of antiquity did not rely on horse and vehicle transport, as services and workplaces were within walking distance. Carlos Moreno's concept of the modern 15-minute city bases many of its ideas on the cities of antiquity.[5] In this case letter, we are focusing on how the healthcare systems can be related to the 15-minute city concept. We would also like to emphasize that this urban concept will also apply to rural areas. For healthcare systems in rural areas, it is conceivable that new levels of care and health services will be introduced. In practice, the first level would focus on basic primary care. The next level can then be a local health centre, where more complex treatment is carried out. At the third level, one can imagine various forms of specialized AI-hospitals with a focus on AI and robotics. This level would be highly specialized and cannot be expected to be within a 15-minute radius. The point of the 15-minute city concept is to think continuously in terms of proximity, compactness, and accessibility for citizens so that their health needs are covered as close to where they live as possible.

The concept of 15-minute cities gained traction after being advocated by Parisian mayor Anne Hidalgo in 2020.[6] Since this first attempt, several cities in Asia, Africa, China, North America, Europe, and other regions, have implemented variations of this concept.[7]

Case letter 2: New organization models while we wait for technological solutions

Rural areas seem to be the first to be affected by shortages of healthcare professionals, and most probably will be the worst affected in the future. This shortage is evident in the lack of applicants for medical and nursing vacancies. Many services in the social care and elderly care sectors are provided on a one-to-one basis. Accordingly, there is currently, and will continue to be, a high demand for "first line competence" in these sectors. It is possible that future technology will provide some assistance, but in any event it will be in these services, where one-to-one relationships currently exist, that future shortages of healthcare personnel will be felt most acutely. Although hospitals are also experiencing difficulties in recruiting enough skilled personnel, it is frontline municipal and regional services that are most severely affected.

There are several factors at play regarding the lack of health personnel. One of the factors that is emerging, and which will be decisive in the future, is the demographic development, as mentioned above. The number of persons aged 80 years or older is expected to increase significantly; this age group will need more healthcare than younger age groups. This development will gain strength in most developed industrial countries between 2020 and 2060.

The demand for labour in the future will become evident in several different sectors; for instance, the transition to a green economy will result in an increased demand in various sectors. In plain language, this may result in shortages regarding labour and expertise. At least, this will be the case before the new technology has been fully implemented in most sectors, i.e., up until the period around 2035–2045, which Kurtzweil terms the Singularity (2005; 2008; 2013). After this period, the new technology will have automated many work operations, so that more labour will become available due to increased productivity. If the above premises are correct, then there will be labour shortages during the period from approximately 2020 up until 2035–2045. In order to deal with this challenge, innovative measures will need to be implemented in this 15–20-year period, especially in the healthcare sector, if the sick and elderly are to get the help they need.

There is little indication that the labour shortage will improve in the next 15–20 years due to future demographic developments. This will become especially acute in the healthcare sector. In order to remedy the lack of "first line competence" (frontline healthcare personnel) during this period, the following measures could be implemented:

1. New organizational forms could be adopted, such as:

   a. The authorities could change the regulations concerning pensions. For example, people should be allowed to receive a full pension while continuing to do paid work; this could ameliorate labour shortages in the healthcare sector in particular. Of course, different countries will have different laws and rules for retirement, but in the main, most countries would be able to benefit from such an organization of pensions and wages.
   b. During the period we are talking about here, the authorities could change the distribution of tasks between different levels in the healthcare sector, so that the workers in the areas where there is enough labour are able to perform work functions that other areas have problems with. This may apply in the hospital sector and also within the primary healthcare services.
   c. The third organizing principle concerns competence. One can imagine that various functional areas that do not require special competence could be filled with another type of competence at a lower level.
   d. The fourth organizing principle is aimed at utilizing existing expertise in other areas that are complementary in relation to the healthcare sector and elderly care. For example, various personnel who work in the nursery and primary school sector could also be assigned tasks in elderly care.

By carrying out these four organizational measures, it will be possible to provide more "first line competence" for the healthcare sector in the time gap during which the new technology has still not yet been fully implemented, which will eventually result in increased automation and a reduction in labour shortage.

Description related to "first line competence"

This chapter addresses the following general research question: How can AI contribute to increasing the number of "first line competence" and improve users'

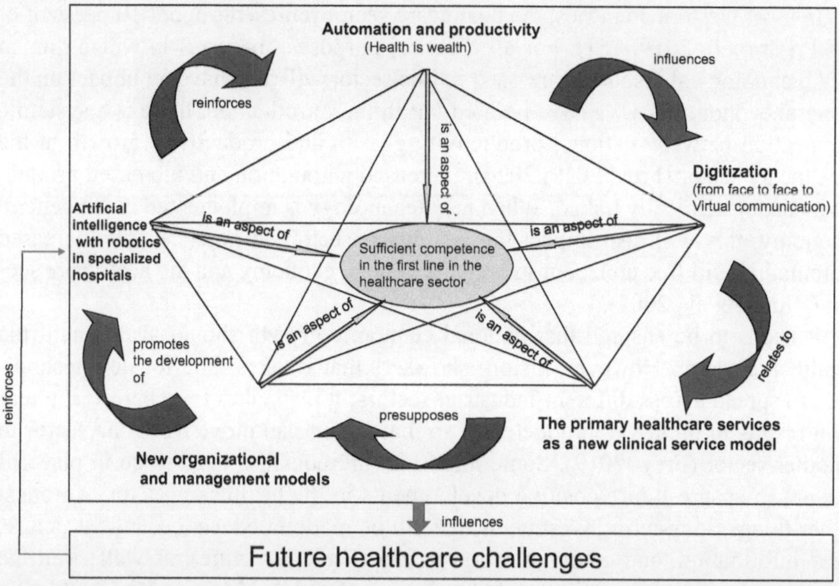

Figure 2.1 "First line competence": A conceptual model.

experience of the healthcare sector? In Figure 2.1 we have developed a conceptual model consisting of five elements relating to how more "first line competence" can be made available in the future. The five elements of the conceptual model are the following:

1. Automation and productivity.
2. Digitalization.
3. The primary healthcare services as a new clinical service model.
4. New organizational and management models.
5. Artificial intelligence and robotics in specialized hospitals.

In the following, we will describe each of these five elements in relation to increasing the number of "first line competence" in the healthcare sector.

Automation and productivity

In the future, it is beyond doubt that artificial intelligence and intelligent robots will promote automation in the general economy.[8] This increase in productivity will reduce labour shortages. For example, in the long term, the workers who lose their jobs in sectors that are to a great extent automated will be able to find work in other sectors such as the healthcare sector. Against this background, increased national productivity will result in redundant labour in one sector of the economy being able to find employment in other sectors, such as the healthcare sector (Al-Turmjan et al., 2022).

In most western countries, the healthcare sector represents about 10 per cent of GDP (Britnell, 2019: 161). For all practical purposes, the ways in which human and technological resources are used in this sector will also have an impact on the general economy. As we have pointed out in the introduction, there is a systemic connection between national productivity growth and productivity growth in the healthcare sector (Frey, 2019; 2020). Increased automation and increased productivity are systemically linked. When new technology is implemented in the general economy, this will also impact the healthcare sector. In practice, this increased automation will free up labour in both the general economy and the healthcare sector (Bloom et al., 2004)..

It needs to be ensured that national economic growth should also benefit the healthcare sector. However, history shows us that it takes time for new technology to spread across different industrial sectors. It also takes time before automation results in improved productivity, so that labour can move from one sector to another sector (Frey, 2019). Some important prerequisites need to be in place, if we are to ensure future positive developments in the healthcare sector. Amongst other things, long-term investments need to be made in education, infrastructure, new information, and communication systems (info-structure), as well as in the digitalization of many activities and processes (Bohr & Memarzadeh, 2020). We also know from history that many projects, such as digitalization projects, will only get off the ground after many mistakes have been made, and new knowledge is developed from experience so that positive developments can be facilitated (Frey, 2020; Mahajan, 2021). As mentioned, we also know that it takes a long time before new technology and methods result in productivity improvements (Solow, 1997). This is often referred to as the "productivity paradox."[9] This was aptly expressed by the Nobel Prize winner in economics, Robert M. Solow (1987: 36), when he said, "I can see the computer age everywhere but in the productivity statistics." This historical insight may be important to keep in mind as we now enter a new technological revolution, driven forward by artificial intelligence. It is probable that there will be many challenges for the various sectors and industries before the productivity growth becomes visible. This will probably apply to the national economy and also to the healthcare sector. Research, learning new ways of producing, new organizational models, and new management models will be needed to ensure that the new technology can deliver increased automation and the expected productivity improvements in the economy as a whole.[10]

It can be expected that in open economies, entrepreneurs introduce new products or services, which may result in substantial improvements in productivity. However, economic history shows us that in the competition between the many entrepreneurs who attempt to find new profit opportunities, many will not succeed and go bankrupt. This development will create challenges and problems for various sectors, such as the healthcare sector. This can already be seen when new information and communication technologies are introduced, because it is often the case that many suppliers and subcontractors go bankrupt.

In plain text, it will often be a case of one step back and two steps forward, regarding the increased automation and productivity that will result from the introduction of new technology. We can also expect to see more public–private partnerships in an attempt to streamline and speed up productivity improvements through the introduction of new AI and robotics applications in the economy as a whole, and especially in the healthcare sector.

Digitalization

The healthcare sector is a global industry with a very large potential regarding digitalization.[11] There are literally millions of employees in this industry. There are 17 million employees in the United States alone. The NHS in the United Kingdom is the world's fifth largest employer.[12] Against this background, it is obvious that the digitalization of the healthcare sector has enormous potential. One of the reasons for the investment in the digitalization of the healthcare sector is that costs are too high and work processes too inefficient from a cost-sustainable perspective. It is hoped that with the implementation of digitalization, then costs can be reduced, productivity increased, and more workers will be available to tackle patient- and care-related tasks. The assumption behind the implementation of digitalization is that more people will be available to make informed and knowledge-based decisions.

There is another aspect of digitalization which can have positive effects in the long term for people's health and health systems. This concerns the fact that people can search for online health information which will increase their knowledge and competence with regard to health decision-making strategies. This development of online health networks is also an aid to health systems in that more people will be able to stay healthy for longer, and thus not need to use healthcare services to such a great extent. In addition, online medical companies offer various services, such as health information and consultations. In this way, more and more people are taking responsibility for their own health.

An important factor regarding the digitalization of healthcare systems is how capable the various systems are at adapting to the new technology, and how quickly the new technology is spread throughout the healthcare sector. It is those systems with the greatest adaptability and speed of diffusion of the new technology that will be able to best implement digitalization, so as to enable an increase in productivity. In order to manage the transition to digitalization of the healthcare sector and to implement AI and robotics solutions, there is much to indicate that this should be a joint task where both the public sector and the private sector work together (Britnell, 2019: 18). This idea of cooperation and co-creation between public and private actors is, among other things, related to the existence of innovation processes in large tech corporations. These large technology companies have, most probably, greater expertise than public health systems, regarding the new innovations and high-tech solutions that can be implemented in the various health systems.

Digitalization has two important purposes in the healthcare sector. First, there is the productivity issue. An increase in productivity will very likely reduce costs. Secondly, digitalization is a precursor to being able to apply new technological innovations, such as IoT, artificial intelligence, and robotics. In this way, digitalization is a necessary, if not sufficient, condition for using the new technology. Without digitalization, it will be almost impossible to adopt artificial intelligence and robotics applications and solutions.

There is also a third factor in addition to productivity and the possibility of using the new technology, which is important in digitalization. The third factor is that extensive digitalization will promote technological learning, which will be necessary, in order to be able to use the new technology. It is assumed that artificial intelligence will be a decisive technology, in order to be at the forefront of the competitive situation that will take place in the global healthcare systems in the future (Al-Turmjan et al., 2022). The competition that exists today will appear archaic compared to the competition that will of necessity develop when artificial intelligence in various forms becomes an important technology in the future healthcare systems (Bohr & Memarzadeh, 2020). The rationale is that only those healthcare systems that can deliver the best quality-assured services will survive, when the new technology has become dominant in the healthcare sector. The point is, then, that the competitive position of healthcare systems is conditioned by the speed with which they can adopt new health-related technological innovations. This competition will have a side effect, which will affect the healthcare workers, and this is that as the healthcare systems compete to deliver the best services, there will emerge a demand for personnel with the appropriate skills. When this demand increases, and the supply of skilled labour does not increase accordingly, simple economic laws will dictate that the salaries of healthcare personnel will increase.

The primary healthcare services as a new clinical service model

It may be interesting to take a look at the cadre of "barefoot doctors" during the Cultural Revolution in China, who provided basic health care for people in rural areas. These "barefoot doctors" formed the crux of the Chinese healthcare system in these areas. The point of this brief historical account is that these doctors had only basic skills after attending brief intensive courses, and could not deal with all the healthcare issues; today, there is still a shortage of properly qualified doctors and nurses in China (Hong, 2021), and there are only a small number of doctors who work in primary healthcare (Britnell, 2019: 47). This is one of the reasons why China is investing in the development of new technology, especially artificial intelligence, in order to promote healthcare services in primary care. The point here is that primary care, both in China and in the West, can learn two things from the history of the "barefoot doctors." The first is that the competence in the primary healthcare service must always be on par with the challenges that it is faced with. In practice, if it is the primary care of patients that is the challenge, then healthcare personnel will need to have such primary care competence. The second lesson is that digitalization and artificial intelligence can be decisive in assisting the help needed in frontline services. In this way, the primary healthcare service can quickly change the quality of the frontline services it delivers. One example that Britnell (2019: 28–29) refers to is Israel. He argues that the primary health care service in Israel has succeeded in what many other countries are aiming to do, namely to make the primary healthcare service the lynchpin of the healthcare sector. In Israel, as in China, the organization around primary healthcare was driven by a historical situation. Later, it has proven to be the pillar that provides people with adequate access to healthcare. In this context, one can here rewrite Ashby's law of requisite variety (Ashby, 1961; 1970; 1981) as follows: Healthcare competences never need to be greater than the challenges faced by healthcare personnel. For all practical purposes, this means that some of the healthcare tasks that were previously allocated to doctors could be transferred to nurses, and those that were only reserved for the nurses could be transferred to auxiliary nurses, and so on.

The two examples above from Israel and China can be said to have influenced much of the development of primary healthcare in the United States and Europe. Development has been spurred by two challenges: cost and competence. In other words, there has been a lack of economic resources and the necessary expertise in the healthcare sector. These challenges were partly solved by introducing a greater focus on primary healthcare service, which could reduce costs. In addition, new investments were made in medium-term healthcare educational programmes for future healthcare workers. This can be related to the above rewriting of Ashby's law: Redesign the healthcare competencies needed in relation to the challenges faced by healthcare personnel.

So one can ask: What does historical knowledge and the above narrative have to do with today's healthcare system? Well, we still face some of the same challenges today. Costs have exploded in the healthcare sector, as shown by, among other things, the examples from the United States and Britain, when we discussed automation and digitalization above. We have also shown above that demographic development creates new challenges for the skills that are needed. In plain language, this means that, as in earlier times, when healthcare was industrialized in the West, it took time before sufficient expertise was available. Something of the same is happening now, when there are more elderly and fewer younger people to take care of the health challenges that the elderly population are faced with. Therefore, the primary healthcare service has once again become a way to cover the health- and care-related needs that are in demand.

Older people living at home have an increasing need to treat various health conditions. These disorders can often be remedied with a care service provided by personnel with short- or medium-term health education. In this way, costs can be reduced, while the competence is at the level that is needed. In other words, patients will not necessarily need a doctor or a fully qualified nurse to provide medication or social care. The level of expertise should always be regulated according to Ashby's law of requisite variety. In practice, this means that the competence must be able to vary according to the needs that exist and not according to a predetermined medical professional norm. This is what also goes under the designation that frontline competence must be changed from "cure to care." In this context, this may mean that one-year and two-year educational programmes in healthcare will be sufficient for the health personnel who deal with the primary care needs of sections of the population.

New organizational and management models

The development of artificial intelligence can be understood in relation to a proximity principle, or the possibility of improving local services. In other words, the necessary expertise needed to serve people's needs should be available to the user in his/her local area. In the initial phase, users of the health services will be able to access services from their own homes. In this way, users will be able to become more active in looking after their own health. For instance, a practical example of this would be to focus more on using technology and local services to keep older people active and healthy. Another example could be to facilitate the increased use of occupational therapists to help older people make their homes safer and more accessible. This will require changed expectations, or a clarification of expectations, in relation to municipal services (such as occupational therapists) and users. It is also conceivable that the various educational programmes will need to be modified and adapted to meet future needs, such as the programmes for occupational therapists, physiotherapists, home nursing, and so on. The point here is to improve resources to enable care in people's homes or in the local area. This can be compared to the transition to home banking where people can now conduct online banking transactions from home rather than at branch locations.

It is the users, i.e., the patients, those in need of care, who will be able to add value to their lives. This may sound somewhat bizarre, but as mentioned above online banking has created value for customers. Digitalization and online banking now mean that users can access banking using a computer, mobile phone, or other device to access services, such as accounts, transferring money, making investments, paying bills, and so on. One can imagine that the new technology will make it possible to reform local healthcare similar to the banking example mentioned above; i.e., users create their own health platforms where they can interact with various therapists and care personnel at a local level. The objection here of course may be that many people will have problems in managing their own health and creating and maintaining the necessary services. To the extent that this will be a problem, local services will need to be developed to enable people to manage online services. In this context, we can envisage the emergence of a new healthcare profession: community therapists.

New organizational models would be able to increase people's empowerment. In relation to healthcare, it will be important to focus more on offering people healthcare services in their local areas. This would be in accordance with the concept of 15-minute cities. Primary care services could be provided to users at healthcare stations, where they can be treated by health personnel with basic competence. This healthcare station can also be imagined as having responsibility for both medical and care tasks. It could also be the case that the individual user was able to make digital contact with the healthcare station, so that the healthcare station personnel could pay home visits. These healthcare stations could satisfy a significant need in local communities, and alleviate pressure in other parts of the healthcare system.

The third step in this new organization could be the local hospitals. These local hospitals could function as health stations providing primary healthcare in the provision of health services, including diagnosis and basic treatment of health conditions. In this context, AI can provide health information in the form of accurate medical diagnoses, that were previously carried out in specialized hospitals. Given such a development in artificial intelligence, which is already underway, these local hospitals will be able to have many medical functions. The local hospitals would then be located in a local area serving between 50,000 and 100,000 users in a city or region. In this way, the proximity principle, cost focus, and expertise could be interrelated and utilized to provide users with services closer to their homes than is the case today.

The fourth step in such a new organization could be thought of as specialized hospitals. These specialized hospitals could take care of many special illnesses, so that those patients with complex illnesses could get the help they needed. These hospitals will utilize new technologies, such as AI and other technologies. They could be organized so that they have a functional and competence collaboration with other specialized hospitals in a defined geographical area. In this way, users could be transferred between the various specialized hospitals where there was free capacity. Consequently, extensive functional collaboration could reduce waiting times and increase productivity in the individual hospitals.

The fifth step in the new organization could be what today is called a "university hospital," i.e., institutions that combine the services of a hospital with medical research in cooperation with a medical university.

Artificial intelligence and robotics in specialized hospitals

Artificial intelligence and robotics have a long history of development, as we have pointed out above. One of the major breakthroughs was when an AI chess machine was able to beat the world's top players. New chess machines were developed based on learning algorithms, which were programmed with the rules of the chess game; by playing against themselves in simulated games, these machines were able to find the best moves. The point of this example is to explain the further development of AI in other fields. It is highly probable that advanced AI, using learning algorithms, will also be further developed in the healthcare industry.

Today, an intelligent robot can, to a certain extent, imitate the cognitive functions of humans. It can learn and then solve problems. In many cases, these intelligent robots can perform many tasks with greater speed and quality than humans can. However, it is the next step in this development that we are referring to here when we talk about specialized AI-powered hospitals that are applying intelligent robots for various tasks. These robots will eventually be able to outcompete humans in the completion of many tasks in specialized hospitals, which will become an integral part of the healthcare systems of the future. Many authors predict that this new technology will become fully integrated with many sectors around 2035–2040 (Johannessen, 2022; 2022a; 2022b; 2022c; 2023a).

It is precisely when new technology becomes an integral part of the specialized areas within hospitals that automation increases. This will lead to increase of labour productivity; the cognitive tasks of workers will to some extent be replaced in some areas by AI and robotics. When this happens, many healthcare personnel will need to find different work tasks. In this context, more "first line competence" will become available who will be able to work where needed within the healthcare sector.

Cognitive capacities that were previously only reserved for humans will, when intelligent robots have developed through their own learning algorithms and through the development of AI engineers, take over specialized tasks in various fields, such as the healthcare sector. This development is already underway, for example in medical diagnosis and in prognoses regarding the development course of a disease. Such intelligent robots will, in many cases, eventually become more skilled in this medical area than health professionals. When this occurs, intelligent robots will transform hospitals into AI-driven hospitals with specialized functional areas, such as cardiovascular illnesses, cancer diagnosis, liver and kidney diseases, and so on.

When the development course of a disease is detected very early, the probability of good prognoses is also greater. Artificial intelligence that can diagnose diseases of the eye, with greater accuracy than medical experts, is already being used. However, robots with this skill are still at an early stage. It is when this technology really takes hold that governments will need to prepare for this transformation in healthcare. In other words, this requires long-term thinking as opposed to short-term thinking. We have already indicated a "long-term" perspective of 2035–2040. Before this period, governments will need to implement new initiatives. This technological development coupled with the increasing demographic bias, at least towards 2060, will make the transformation in the healthcare sector absolutely necessary. However, this transformation will not occur by itself, and it will take a long time to prepare if all levels in the healthcare sector will have the time to keep up with the change processes. This is why the changes need to be initiated in the very near future, before it is too late to turn this giant global industry around.

We need to become aware of the fact that AI robots will become a part of everyday reality in the not-so-distant future. As mentioned above, AI and robotics are already being utilized in our hospitals. These intelligent robots will also exist in various sizes and formats; for example, in the field of nanotechnology, where "nanobots" can be used to clear clogged arteries. In contrast, one can imagine large intelligent machines, similar to CT scanning machines. However, these new AI-powered machines will be able to carry out diagnoses and provide treatment options in a few seconds after the images have been scanned. In our context, the point is that these new machines will increase the quality of treatment, and also promote automation, making more "first line competence" available. Our point here is not to say specifically what the future organization of healthcare will look like, but only to suggest some alternatives when the new technology becomes a fact.

Based on the description in this section, we have developed a conceptual model that shows aspects of how more "first line competence" will become available in the future healthcare system.

Analysis related to "first line competence" in the healthcare sector

We have argued above that more "first line competence" will be available within the healthcare sector, when AI becomes an operative part of the sector. This opportunity will be realized when the new technology increases automation and digitalization, which will free up labour, resolving labour shortages within the economy in general, but also within the healthcare sector in particular. It has also been argued that it will take some years before the new technology is able to free up this human labour. It is during this period of time that the healthcare sector will face challenges, because temporary solutions will need to be found to remedy the increased demand for "first line competence."

Based on the premises described in the introduction to this analysis, governments will need to adopt two parallel strategies. A short-term strategy until sometime around 2035–2040, and a longer-term strategy for the period after 2035–2040, when artificial intelligence and intelligent robots have become fully integrated into the economic system.

Liu et al.[13] have concluded from a survey that by 2030 there will be a global demand of around 80 million health workers. It is also estimated by the World Health Organization (WHO) that there will be a global shortage of 15 million health workers during the same period.[14]Such a projection regarding the shortage of health workers will hopefully become something that governments will attempt to rectify by preparing for such a scenario. However, it should also be pointed out that the labour shortage referred to above is for 2030; from the present day up until this period, shortages will be less acute. If we assume that the new technology will be gradually phased into the economy in general, and the healthcare sector in particular, automation processes will free up labour, so more "first line competence" will become available in the healthcare sector. In other words, as we move towards 2030–2040, the shortage of health workers will become less and less. This assumption is based on the fact that general-purpose technologies tend to increase automation and productivity and free up human labour, which then becomes available in the various sectors of the economy (Frey, 2019; 2020; Bessen, 2020).

In this analysis, and in this chapter, we argue that labour productivity is the most important factor that government authorities need to focus on, because increased productivity will improve people's access to health, and make available more "first line competence" in the healthcare sector. However, in the interim period, until the new technology is fully introduced, a possible strategy for making more "first line competence" available would be to adopt alternative ways of thinking, regarding the levels of competence that are needed in relation to different work tasks in different parts of the healthcare sector. We know this is a complicated and difficult debate. Nonetheless, we believe it is absolutely crucial to adopt new ways of thinking, in order to address the shortage of health workers as we move towards 2030. What we suggest here is increased health workforce flexibility. Specifically, this can be achieved in relation to the levels of competencies needed and the distribution of work tasks. For example, to overcome recruitment problems, educational requirements can be adjusted for certain healthcare positions. In addition, task shifting and task sharing can be increased so that health workers are able to complete multiple work tasks in different areas. We will not elaborate specifically on what this may involve, because this is beyond the scope of this book. However, we can suggest some examples, such as task shifting between physicians and nurses, whereby nurses carry out some of the tasks traditionally done by doctors. In other words, the division of labour in healthcare is often governed by historical tradition, rather than present-day medical needs. Similarly, this could also apply to the division of labour between nurses and assistant nurses. In many instances, it could be productive to review the work tasks of these two groups of health workers in relation to the nature of tasks and competence requirements. The above suggestions may be one way to solve the shortage of health workers as we move towards 2030.

The point is that if we do not adopt some changes regarding the work tasks of the various health workers, then we risk having a growing shortage of labour, at least until the new technology is phased-in, in the various areas and levels in the healthcare sector.

The apparent paradox that the creation of more "first line competence" is dependent on the integration of "cold intelligent machines" in the healthcare sector is interesting. In other words, more "first line competence" will become available when new technology automates many tasks, freeing up labour that can be utilized elsewhere, for example, in frontline healthcare. In many countries around the world, demographic developments are being discussed as a problem regarding the predicted future shortage of health workers around 2030.[15] However, if one takes a more dynamic technological perspective than the aforementioned survey, then it may be possible that artificial intelligence and intelligent robots, as well as the qualitative reorganization of the health systems, in terms of the distribution of work functions, and the utilization of expertise, will be able to provide the "first line competence" that will be needed in the healthcare sector. The point, however, is that there are different perspectives before and after the introduction of artificial intelligence, not only in the health systems, but also in the economy in general. This insight is not based on assumptions about an uncertain future, but on the knowledge of economic history. One can always argue that this time it will be different. The only question is why it should be different in the Fourth Industrial Revolution than in the previous three. In the previous three industrial revolutions, new technology automated away many jobs, but also created many more jobs than those eliminated by automation. There are a few things that indicate that it will be different this time.

Many of the investigations that are conducted regarding future health challenges are concerned with, and are limited to, how to secure more health personnel. If one has such a perspective, and largely projects developments based on the view that production and organizational frameworks will more or less remain the same, then the picture of healthcare in the future looks bleak. Therefore, it is not unimportant which methods, and technological and organizational perspectives, are adopted, when future health challenges are being discussed.

It may sound incongruous to say that the health sector has a lot to learn from automobile production and other industrial production of goods and services. The point in our context is that the high-tech industries of today have embraced artificial intelligence and digitalization, as well as changing forms of organization and management. It is against this background that the health sector can learn a lot from the high-tech industries, which have developed new methods of production, such as in the production of modern automobiles. The automotive industry has greatly changed in recent years. Amongst other things, AI is assisting vehicles to become more aware of their surroundings and make optimal decisions to avoid accidents.

Globalization from the 1980s until the 2020s has led to a transfer of expertise between different geographical areas and between different industries. It is against this background that one can assume that the development of methods used in the production of automobiles can be transferred to the development of the future health system. The rationale is that both high-tech production and healthcare production are based on the same categories. The categories are technology, competence, management, and organization (Liker, 2008; 2020). Industries, such as the automotive industry, provide countries with economic security; on the other hand, health systems provide people with health security. Against this background, one can envisage benchmarking occurring between high-tech industrial systems that ensure economic security, and the health systems that ensure people's health security.

Social cohesion concerns the strength of relationships and the feeling of solidarity among members of a community or country. Both economic and health security are important for social cohesion. It is also against this background that one can say that "health is wealth." By this we mean that the prosperity of a country is not only a result of economic value creation but is largely conditioned by the well-being and security the population experiences from having a well-functioning health system.

Artificial intelligence in the healthcare sector will not only reduce costs and increase productivity but also improve the quality of services, in relation to more accurate and safer diagnoses and treatments. In addition, artificial intelligence will be able to ensure a longer life, with better well-being in terms of health (Woods, 2020).

There is much talk about the "digital doctor" of the future (Wachter, 2015), and how artificial intelligence can help the medical profession at all levels (Bohr & Memarzadeh, 2020). Automation and digitalization, as well as the future AI-powered hospitals, will largely solve the current shortage of healthcare personnel. However, health services, and the use of new technology, will vary according to country and region. In other words, it is probable that central urban areas will first apply the new technologies, but less so in rural areas. Against this background, the organization and new management models will be decisive in achieving good health systems for all the citizens of a country.

As mentioned above, demographic developments will result in an ageing population, and fewer younger people who are able to take care of an elderly population. Moreover, many of the health workers will also reach retirement age. This will require a reorganization of the healthcare sector to tackle this problem. This challenge can be solved in several ways. As mentioned, the introduction of new technology in the future will partly solve this problem. Another solution would be to motivate those health workers who have reached retirement age to work longer than they had originally intended. This solution will need to be implemented at the government level; i.e., policies would have to be introduced providing incentives for workers who choose to work beyond retirement age. Tax breaks and higher wages could be two types of incentives. In addition, pensions should not be reduced if workers choose to continue working. A combination of the above proposals would perhaps be the best way to motivate people to work a few extra years beyond retirement age.

In addition to the above measures to solve labour shortages in healthcare, it will perhaps also be important to reflect on how educational programmes can be designed to meet the health needs of the future. As mentioned above, shorter and more generalist educational programmes could be introduced; these would qualify people to work as care workers for the elderly. This will be necessary both before and after the new technology is fully integrated into the healthcare system. This will be due to the fact that demographic changes will result in more elderly needing care, as well as due to the fact that many health personnel will have reached retirement age. We therefore propose a two-pronged approach: Health personnel should be encouraged to work beyond retirement age, by offering various incentives, and new health educational programmes will need to be designed to qualify people who can meet the needs of an ageing population.

It is possible that the large shortage of medical specialists can be solved to some extent by the use of artificial intelligence and intelligent robots. However, it is unlikely that the new technology will be able to significantly reduce the demand for care workers in elderly care. Admittedly, robots can be used for the heavy lifts of patients, to ease the jobs of nurses, but there will still be a large demand for care workers.

It is also highly likely that there will be an increasing demand for speciality doctors as the population ages. If this demand increases, then it is probable that new AI and robotics technology will not be able to solve this increased demand. If this becomes a reality, then new organizational and management models would be a significant contribution to solving this challenge.

Theoretical reflections related to "first line competence" in the healthcare sector

There are two variables we focus on in this theoretical approach. The first is the degree of application of AI and intelligent robots in hospitals. The second is the degree of focus on primary healthcare. The four propositions derived from the typology in Figure 2.2 form a mini theory for "first line competence," related to the application of AI and intelligent robots in hospitals, as well as the degree of focus and development of the primary healthcare service. "Theory" here refers to "a system of propositions" (Bunge, 1974: v).

The four propositions that we have developed in relation to these two variables are given below.

Proposition 1: The greater the degree of application of AI and intelligent robots that takes place in hospitals, and the greater the degree of focus there is on the primary

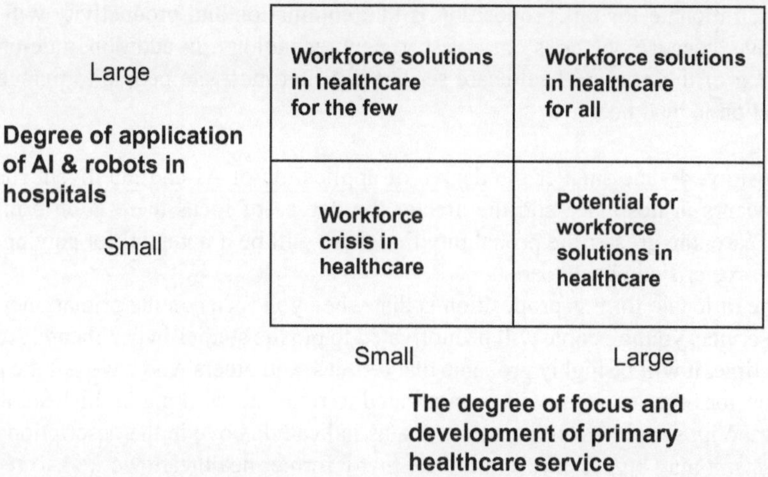

Figure 2.2 "First line competence" in the healthcare sector: A typology.

healthcare service, the greater the probability of solving the challenges related to providing enough "first line competence" in the healthcare sector.

The rationale for this proposition is that AI and intelligent robots will increase automation and productivity in the entire sector, thereby freeing up labour for the frontline, where patients need "first line competence" care. There is a prerequisite for this proposition, and that is that the new technology also increases automation and productivity in other sectors of the economy.

Proposition 2: The greater the degree of application of AI and intelligent robots that takes place in hospitals, and the less degree of focus there is on the primary healthcare service, the greater the probability of solving the challenges related to providing "first line competence" in the healthcare sector, but mainly for those who can pay for healthcare.

The rationale for this proposition is that the emphasis on artificial intelligence and intelligent robots in hospitals will free up "first line competence" in specialized hospitals. The point, however, is that when you invest little in the primary healthcare service, the possibility and probability that it will be those with the greatest financial resources who will be able to pay for treatment increases. The assumption in this proposition is that the primary healthcare service is to a great extent a service provided for the general population. When this service is de-prioritized, relatively speaking, it will be those with good finances who will be able to pay for healthcare at the specialized hospitals.

Proposition 3: The less the degree of application of AI and intelligent robots that occurs in hospitals, and the less degree of focus there is on primary healthcare, the greater the likelihood that a workforce crisis in healthcare will develop.

The rationale for this proposition is that automation and productivity will not improve, because one does not invest in new technology. In addition, a de-prioritization of the primary healthcare service will not motivate people to pursue an education in healthcare.

Proposition 4: The smaller the degree of application of AI and intelligent robots that occurs in hospitals, and the greater the degree of focus there is on primary healthcare, the greater the probability that there will be a potential for solving the workforce crisis in healthcare.

The rationale for this proposition is that when you focus on the primary healthcare service, young people will be motivated to pursue studies in healthcare. At the same time, it will be highly probable that retirees, and others who have left the profession for other reasons, will be motivated to return to working in the healthcare sector. With simple incentive structures, as indicated above in the description and analysis, it may be possible to motivate many former healthcare workers to return to working in the healthcare sector. This will provide more "first line competence" for those who need them.

Based on the above narratives, description, analysis, and argumentation related to the four propositions, we have developed a typology regarding providing enough "first line competence" in the healthcare sector.

Practical utility related to "first line competence" in the healthcare sector

Improvements in people's health are not just a matter of individual well-being. People's health is directly related to increased economic growth. Research shows that an average increase in life expectancy of one year leads to an increase in economic growth of 4% (Bloom et al., 2004: 1–13).

Against this background, investment in people's health is directly linked to a country's opportunities for economic development and progress. This provides clear guidance that investment in artificial intelligence and other high technology in the healthcare sector is not only crucial for people's well-being and welfare but also for national economic growth. Investment and new applications of AI in the healthcare sector will increase automation and productivity (Al-Turmjan et al., 2022; Bohr & Memarzadeh, 2020). As previously described, automation in the healthcare sector will lead to more people having to find other work tasks, but not necessarily outside the healthcare sector. Of course, this does not mean that doctors and nurses will have to be retrained and find work in other sectors. For these two occupational groups, of which there is a deficit throughout the entire healthcare sector in most countries, this development will result in a better balance between supply and demand.

For the individual hospital, artificial intelligence and intelligent robots will promote the development of the robotic hospital. This must not be perceived as a hospital without human competencies. The point is simply that many of the work operations in a specialized robotics-operated hospital are carried out with the help of artificial intelligence that is used in various health-related technologies (Mahajan, 2021: 324–516).

Hospitals are of course not production facilities, such as factories that produce cars. Let this be absolutely clear, even though we have previously compared some production models from the car industry with the production of health in the healthcare sector. The point of what we have previously mentioned is that you can learn from other industries, even if one industry is qualitatively different from another. Hospitals and the healthcare sector are special in the sense that it involves people taking care of other people. Having said this, this does not mean that intelligent robots cannot robotize parts of the work processes in hospitals. For example, when doctors perform eye surgery, AI can greatly assist such operations. However, this does not mean that the patient should not be able to communicate with a health professional who can provide information regarding such an operation, it just means that AI can be applied when the complexity of operations is great.

Human competence becomes particularly important when the development course of an illness has multiple causal reasons, and where there are multiple conditions that the patient is suffering from. In plain language, when the complexity of an illness increases, so does the need to be looked after by "first line competence." An important point is that even if "cold hands," i.e., robotization using AI, can provide better qualitative results over a longer time perspective, there will still be a need for "first line competence," especially when the complexity of an illness is great. In particular, the complexity of illnesses will increase with an ageing population. In this situation, there will also be a greater need for "first line competence," i.e., healthcare workers with a human touch who can show empathy. It is in this context that one might say that "humans are underrated" (Colvin, 2015).

In particular, the above will apply in the primary healthcare service. This is where the individual patient can meet a health professional with expertise, who can show care and empathy for the patient's situation. Care and empathy are not qualities that characterize AI and robotics. This technology is characterized by rationality, logical reasoning, statistical filtering, mathematical regularity, and so on, but not empathy, and social and emotional intelligence. It is in this context that human expertise will be preferable. This will probably also apply in the future. By investing in the primary healthcare service, both in terms of competence, salary, and status, the probability will increase that more people will pursue healthcare studies. This will eventually provide more healthcare workers in the future.

Most healthcare systems are labour-intensive. This does not mean that it has to be this way forever. Artificial intelligence and intelligent robots will probably reduce the need for labour in some areas of the healthcare sector. On the other hand, the ageing populations of industrialized countries will create an increased need for healthcare workers. Thus, even though the new technology will be able to carry out many work tasks, there will also be an increasing need for "first line competence" in the healthcare sector. Therefore, investments will still be needed in healthcare education, in order to meet future needs. As we have discussed previously, there will also be a need to increase the differentiation of competencies needed in the various functional areas. For example, it may be suitable to establish studies of shorter duration, such as one- and two-year programmes. In other words, this concerns adapting competencies to the work functions that need to be carried out, more specifically creating more "first line competence" for the primary healthcare service.

In addition to the new function-adapted competence areas, there will also be a need for qualitatively new functions in the healthcare sector. These new functions will be related to the new technology. Artificial intelligence and intelligent robots require that there will also have to be competence within the healthcare sector that is compatible with the new technology. Technological competence within the healthcare sector is nothing new. The new thing is that it is highly likely that the demand for this new technological competence will increase considerably. One can envision that nurses and doctors will have this competence. In practice, this will take a long time. For all practical purposes, this competence will be compatible with the new technology; i.e., a distinctive competence related to operating, coding, and developing artificial intelligence applications used in the healthcare sector. In contrast, one could imagine that professionals with technological competence worked in teams with medical professionals. This could involve work functions such as X-rays, diagnoses, and analysis.

There is an interesting connection between the development in the labour-intensive aspects of the healthcare sector and in the economy in general. The costs related to labour are relatively greater in the healthcare sector than in the economy as a whole (Britnell, 2019). This indicates that labour productivity in the healthcare sector is lower than in the rest of the economy.[16] This may mean that there is more need for workers with the human touch in the healthcare sector than in other sectors. However, it may also mean that the healthcare sector is more technologically conservative than other sectors. In reality, it is probably a mixture of these two factors. It is the spread and application of innovations, in general, and technological innovations in particular, that will largely determine whether the healthcare sector adopts new technology (Rogers, 2003). Surveys have been carried out in England which show that there is greater resistance to the investment and application of new technology in the healthcare sector than in other sectors.[17] If this is a general tendency around the world, then this represents a challenge for the healthcare sector, because there is a clear connection between new technology and labour productivity.

It is the organizations, regardless of whether they are within the healthcare sector or in other industries, that are furthest ahead in the application of new technology, that will have the best conditions to become leaders in the international competition. It is therefore crucial for the healthcare sector, at various levels, that efforts are made to adopt different types of new technology. In its consequences, this will increase work productivity and thus provide more "first line competence" for the various functional areas and at different levels within the healthcare sector.

On the basis of the above description, narratives, analysis, theoretical reflection, and practical utility, we have developed a Boudon–Coleman diagram (Figure 2.3) for facilitating more "first line competence" in the healthcare sector.

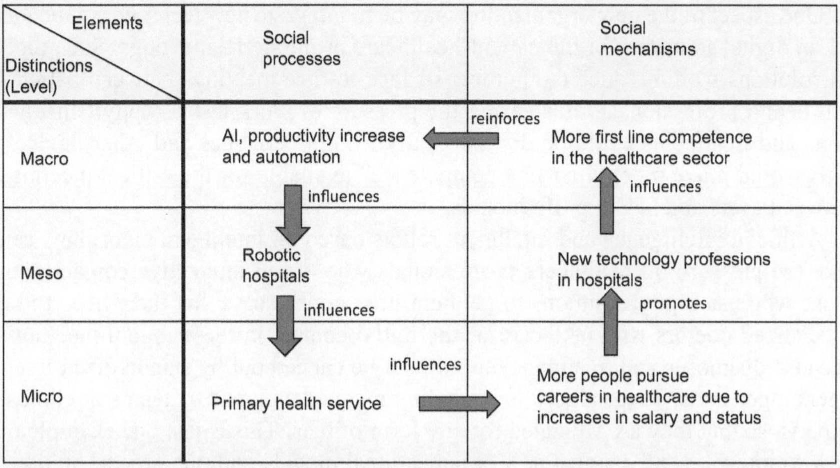

Figure 2.3 "First line competence": A Boudon–Coleman diagram.

Conclusion

Good population health is essential for prosperity and well-being. It is against this background that one can say that "health is wealth." In order to create population health, it is crucial to secure enough personnel with the right skills at the various levels in the various health systems. Important in this context are those health workers who work closest to the patient, the so-called "first line competence," care workers with the human touch, who can ensure people's well-being. To achieve enough of these care workers, there are many measures that governments can implement. One of these measures is to invest sufficiently in new technology, such as AI and robotics. This may seem paradoxical, because "cold" technology is not associated with "first line competence." However, the application of new technology and increased automation will free up labour so that more "first line competence" will be available. In order to implement new technology in the health sector it is crucial that 5G (and later 6G) networks have been developed to facilitate digitalization that will enable the application of new technology. In other words, investment in new technology, and efficient networks to enable optimal digitalization, will promote the automation of work functions and make more labour available in the healthcare sector.

Creating more "first line competence" in the healthcare sector is not just a matter of increasing automation and productivity, in order to free up labour. It is just as important to be innovative in other areas, such as organization. In this context, it is important to transform primary healthcare into an efficient and productive service model that is client-oriented, in the same way businesses are customer-oriented. The introduction of such a service model will require legislation. In addition to this focus on a client-oriented service model, new organization and management models will be needed to free up "first line competence" for frontline healthcare tasks.

One aspect of the new organization may be to integrate new technology, such as AI, in digital solutions for the patient-healthcare professional meetings. Such digital solutions would reduce the number of face-to-face meetings between patients and health professionals, thus easing the pressure of work tasks. Many consultations and treatments could be done digitally using telephones and other devices. This would make more "first line competence" available for the critical meetings between users and health professionals.

Artificial intelligence and intelligent robots based on intelligent algorithms can take the pressure off healthcare professionals who are in interactive contact with those who use digital solutions to get help. It is not the case that there need to be specialized doctors who take care of the initial contact in these digital meetings, because diagnoses and treatment can initially be carried out by standardized intelligent algorithms. These algorithms may in time be developed by teams of clinical experts, so that they are validated for any form of bias. This is just one example of how to integrate and connect new organizational models with the new technology to promote the quality of the innovative organizational models in the healthcare sector.

By using the new technology in relatively basic organizational models to promote service to users, one can in a simple and cost-saving way increase accessibility, satisfaction, and the perceived and real quality in the first encounter with the primary healthcare service.

Throughout this chapter, we have focused on how AI can create more "first line competence" and increase the perceived quality in the healthcare sector. In this conclusion, we have tried to show that the application of new technology and digital solutions can increase automation and productivity and automation, and

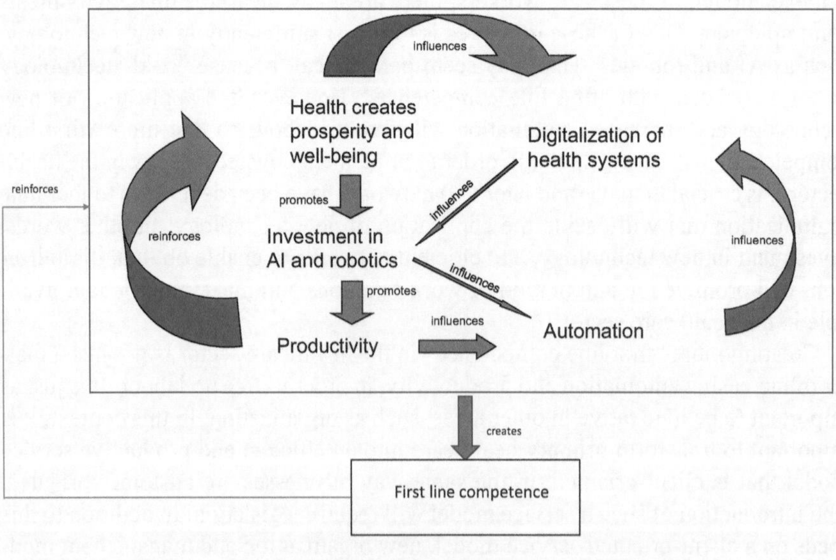

Figure 2.4 Systemic relationships in the healthcare sector: A loop diagram.

consequently free up "first line competence," which can be used in the critical meetings between users and health professionals.

In relation to the general research question we have investigated in this chapter, and based on the above narratives, description, analysis, theoretical reflections, and the practical utility, we have developed a loop diagram to show the systemic relationships in the healthcare sector (Figure 2.4).

Notes

1 https://en.wikipedia.org/wiki/Carlos_Moreno_(urbanist)
2 https://en.wikipedia.org/wiki/15-minute_city
3 https://en.wikipedia.org/wiki/15-minute_city
4 https://en.wikipedia.org/wiki/15-minute_city
5 https://en.wikipedia.org/wiki/15-minute_city
6 https://en.wikipedia.org/wiki/Anne_Hidalgo
7 https://en.wikipedia.org/wiki/15-minute_city#Implementations
8 Autor, 2015; Eubanks, 2017; Frey, 2019; 2020; Johannessen, 2020; 2020a; 2020b; 2021; 2023; Johannessen & Sætersdal, 2020; Leontief, 1986; Simon, 1965; Skidelsky & Craig, 2020; Susskind, 2020.
9 https://en.wikipedia.org/wiki/Robert_Solow
10 Antonelli, 2009; Brynjolfsson & Saunders, 2013; Chesbrough, 2003; Ford, 2016; Ford, 2021; Frey, 2019; Habakkuk, 1962; Susskind, 2020; Susskind, J., 2018.
11 https://www.medesk.net/en/blog/2017-04-27-deloitte-analytics/
12 https://www.bbc.com/news/magazine-17429786
13 https://human-resources-health.biomedcentral.com/articles/10.1186/s12960-017-0187-2
14 https://human-resources-health.biomedcentral.com/articles/10.1186/s12960-017-0187-2 https://www.who.int/news/item/02-06-2022-global-strategy-on-human-resources-for-health--workforce-2030
15 https://human-resources-health.biomedcentral.com/articles/10.1186/s12960-017-0187-2 https://www.who.int/news/item/02-06-2022-global-strategy-on-human-resources-for-health--workforce-2030
16 https://www.kingsfund.org.uk/publications/innovation-nhs
17 https://www.kingsfund.org.uk/publications/innovation-nhs

References

Al-Turmjan, F.; Kumar, M.; Staphany, T. & Bhardwaj, A. (2022). *Evolving role of AI and IoMT in the health care market*, Springer, London.

Antonelli, C. (2009). The economics of innovation: from the classical legacies to the economics of complexity, *Economics of Innovation and New Technology*, 18(7), 611–646, http://doi.org/10.1080/10438590802564543. To link to this article: http://doi.org/10.1080/10438590802564543.

Ashby, W.R. (1961). *An introduction to cybernetics*, Chapman & Hall LTD, New York.

Ashby, W.R. (1970). Connectance of large dynamic (cybernetic) systems: Critical values for stability, *Nature*, 228(5273, 21 November), 784–785.

Ashby, W.R. (1981). What is an Intelligent Machine? in Conant, R. (ed.), *Mechanisms of intelligence*, pp. 231–278. Intersystems Seaside, New York.

Autor, D. (2015). Why are there still so many jobs? The history and future of workplace automation, *Journal of Economic Perspectives*, 29(3), 3–30.

Bessen, J. (2020). Attitudes to technology: Part 1, in Skidelsky, R. & Craig, N. (eds.), *Work in the future*, Palgrave, London, pp. 83–88.

Bloom, D.E.; Canning, D. & Sevilla, J. (2004). The effect of health on economic growth: A production function approach, *World Development*, 32, 1–13.
Bohr, A. & Memarzadeh, K. (2020). *Artificial intelligence in healthcare*, Academic Press, New York.
Britnell, M. (2019). *Human: Solving the global workforce crises in healthcare*, Oxford University Press, Oxford.
Brynjolfsson, E. & Saunders, A. (2013). *Wired for innovation: How information technology is reshaping the economy*, The MIT Press, London.
Bunge, M. (1974). *Sense and reference*, Reidel, Dordrecht.
Chesbrough, H.W. (2003). *Open innovation: The new imperative for creating and profiting from technology*, Harvard Business School press, Boston.
Colvin, G. (2015). *Humans are underrated: What high achievers know that brilliant machines never will*, Nicolas Brealey, London.
Eubanks, V. (2017). *Automating inequality*, St. Martin's Press, New York.
Ford, M. (2016). *The rise of the robotics, Technology and the threat of mass unemployment*, Oneworld, New York.
Ford, M. (2021). *Rule of the robots*, Basic Book, London.
Frey, C.B. (2019). *The technology trap: Capital, labor, and power in the age of automation*, Princeton University Press, Princeton.
Frey, C.B. (2020). Attitudes towards technology: Part II, in Skidelsky, R. & Craig, N. (eds.), *Work in the future: The automation revolution*, Palgrave, London, pp. 89–97.
Habakkuk, J. (1962). *American and British technology in the nineteenth century, the search for labor savings inventions*, Cambridge University Press, Cambridge.
Hong, L. (2021). *China in one village: The history of one town and the future of the world*, Verso, London.
Johannessen, J-A. (2020). *The workplace of the future*, Routledge, London.
Johannessen, J-A. (2020a). *Automation, innovation and economic crises: Survival the fourth industrial revolution*, Routledge, London.
Johannessen, J-A. (2020b). *Artificial intelligence, automation and the future of competence at work*, Routledge.
Johannessen, J-A. (2021). *Artificial intelligence, automation and ethics in the innovation economy*, Routledge, London.
Johannessen, J-A. (2022). *The philosophy of tacit knowledge*, Emerald, London.
Johannessen, J-A. (2022a). *A systemic approach to continuous change in the innovation economy*, Routledge, London.
Johannessen, J-A. (2022b). *Intelligent robots consciousness and creativity: The search for hidden knowledge, The cognitive side of knowledge management*, Emerald, London.
Johannessen, J-A. (2022c). *Creativity, innovation and the fourth industrial revolution: The da Vinci strategy*, Routledge, London.
Johannessen, J-A. (2023). *Artificial intelligence and creativity: Implications for automation in the innovation economy*, Routledge, London.
Johannessen, J-A. (2023a). *The fourth industrial revolution and the labour market: Future proofing work in the innovation economy*, Routledge, London.
Johannessen, J-A. & Sætersdal, H. (2020). *Automation, innovation and work*, Routledge, London.
Kurzweil, R. (2005). *The singularity is near*, Penguin, London.
Kurzweil, R. (2008). *The age of spiritual machines: When computers exceed human intelligence*, Penguin, London.
Kurzweil, R. (2013). *How to create a mind: The secret of human thought revealed*, Penguin Books, New York.
Leontief, W. (1986). *The future impact of automation on workers*, Oxford University Press, Oxford.
Liker, J. (2008). *Toyota culture: The heart and soul of the Toyota way*, McGraw Hill, New York.

Liker, J. (2020). *The Toyota way*, McGraw-Hill, New York.

Mahajan, P.S. (2021). *Artificial intelligence in healthcare*, MedMantra, New Mexico.

Rogers, E.M. (2003). *Diffusion of innovations*, Free Press, New York.

Simon, H.A. (1965). *The shape of automation for men and management*, New York: Harper & Row.

Skidelsky, R. & Craig, N. (2020). Introduction, in Skidelsky, R. & Craig, N. *Work in the future: The automation revolution*, Palgrave, London, pp. 1–7.

Solow, R.M. (1987). Review of S.S. Cohen and J. Zysman, "Manufacturing matters: The myth of the post-industrial economy". *New York Times Book Review*, 12 July, 36.

Solow, R.M. (1997). *Learning from learning by doing: Lessons for economic growth*, Stanford University Press, Stanford.

Susskind, D. (2020). *A world without work: Technology, automation and how we should respond*, Allen Lane, London.

Susskind, J. (2018). *Living together in a world transformed by technology*, Oxford University Press, Oxford.

Wachter, R. (2015). *The digital doctor*, McGraw Hill, New York.

Woods, T. (2020). *Live longer with AI*, Packt, Birmingham.

3 AI and opportunities in the healthcare sector

Core idea

- The application of artificial intelligence (AI) in the healthcare sector is increasing the automation of work processes, resulting in increased productivity, and increased quality in analyses, diagnoses, and treatment.

Key points

- The use of AI in medical applications will be characterized by the uncovering of patterns and the prediction of future pattern developments.
- Our view is that the increased application of AI technology in the healthcare sector will lead to an increase in the use of hands-on staff.
- The following six areas are systemically linked and are crucial for increasing the productivity of healthcare workers:

  1. Focus on what the system is designed to do.
  2. Pay attention to results.
  3. Focus on the development of innovations.
  4. Reward knowledge sharing.
  5. Facilitate the self-organization of employees, teams, and departments allowing them to identify the most efficient path for goal achievement.
  6. Facilitate the continuous development of competencies.

- A qualitatively new profession will become part of surgical teams. These professionals will have expertise in the use of AI and the high-tech tools used in surgical operations.
- The further development of AI in clinical practices will result in the technology being used to replace work functions that were previously carried out by health personnel.
- New technology is becoming more affordable, but healthcare costs are sharply increasing.
- The increased application of AI technology will lead to an increase in the use of hands-on staff.

DOI: 10.4324/9781003497325-4

Introduction

In this chapter, we will examine the following question: What are the opportunities for using Artificial intelligence (AI) in the healthcare sector? To exemplify this issue, we have made extensive use of case letters. There are five general challenges regarding the use of AI in the healthcare sector: "mobile healthcare"; the productivity of healthcare workers; a greater focus on healthcare workers; life expectancy and a qualitative improvement of people's lives; and the importance of the view that humans are underrated, despite the advancements in new technology.[1]

An important point regarding the use of AI in the healthcare sector is that the knowledge base of medical science is being increasingly separated into different professional sectors. To put it another way, there is increasingly less emphasis on the skills of general practitioners and non-specialized nurses, while the fragmentation of technological professional competence has come more and more into focus. Of course this is nothing new, for a century and more, when new medical knowledge has been introduced, generalists have been increasingly segmented into specialty areas. The point in our context though, regarding the use of AI, is that specialization is being increasingly put into a technological system. It is often the case that health practitioners lose an overview of the capability and extent of technological applications in the healthcare sector, due to the increasing complexity (Saxena et al., 2021; Esposito, 2022).

Practising medicine at different levels becomes qualitatively different when AI becomes an integral part of medical treatment. One feature that may be interesting to note is that AI can integrate the doctor–patient relationship into something similar to the old model where doctors made house calls. This analogy, however, has a modern twist though. The use of "mobile health services" will not mean the use of house calls but the possibility of providing individualized services "virtually," i.e., where medical services can be delivered remotely. Using mobile solutions that utilize AI will enable doctors and medical professionals to provide a service model that focuses on the needs of the individual patient. In other words, although the use of AI in the healthcare sector has resulted in an increased segmentation regarding speciality areas, AI can also be utilized to integrate these specialized skills into a mobile health design model. This represents developments that can increase the performance of healthcare workers, because they will be able to utilize AI support that will enable them to increase their productivity, while also increasing the quality of services provided. In other words, the use of AI will enable health professionals to perform qualitatively better services. From a longer perspective, this will most probably lead to qualitative improvements in people's lives and increased life expectancy due to the fact that people will have rapid access to qualified medical help. However, it should be noted that although AI will become more important in the provision of medical services, regarding examinations, diagnosis, and treatment, there will also be a great need for qualified medical personnel. In other words, the competencies of humans should not be underrated in this process.

Information technology led to many breakthroughs in medical practices. The development of 5G and 6G networks is most probably a prerequisite for the effective functioning of AI and robotics applications. Most OECD countries are already developing 5G networks; in addition, China has also invested heavily in developing 5G networks (Johannessen, 2021; 2022). In the future, these new networks coupled with AI applications will most probably facilitate an expansion of mobile healthcare services, where primary healthcare professionals will be able to increase their productivity and improve the quality of services. With the aforementioned development and a greater degree of AI user-friendliness, health professionals will function as digital knowledge workers in the primary healthcare services. This increased focus on frontline health professionals, and a new and user-friendly technology, will most probably, from a longer perspective, improve patients' quality of life and increase their life expectancy.

Although new AI technology will be able to solve many future challenges in the primary healthcare services and in specialized hospitals, people with medical and caring skills will still be needed to perform the work functions that are crucial for people's welfare. Therefore, it may also be said that AI is a necessary prerequisite for promoting the care of patients in the future. However, it should be noted that this technology alone will not be sufficient to ensure efficient healthcare. It is the interaction between AI applications and human competencies that will be crucial for improving and developing healthcare services.

We have pointed out several times in this book that it is in the period where AI is being adopted and until the time that the technology has fully become part of how the health system works, that we will be in a so-called "in-between moment." It is during this period of time that we will see a situation where we thought technology would solve most problems, but that we nevertheless still have challenges and problems in applying the new technology. This insight is nothing new. It has characterized all the previous technological revolutions (Frey, 2019; 2020).

Our enthusiasm related to the future development of healthcare services utilizing AI should be viewed from a slightly longer-term perspective. In other words, the full development of AI applications within the healthcare sector will take place when we reach the "Singularity," which Kurzweil suggests will occur in 2035–2040. "Singularity" is when machine intelligence surpasses human intelligence, at least in relation to logical and rational intelligence (Kurzweil, 2005; 2008; 2013). In the interim period, people's expectations will most probably be set too high regarding the applications of the new technology. In order to fully utilize AI in healthcare, we will have to invest a lot in learning how to use this technology for the various systems in the healthcare sector. We should also expect that many of the projects that will be launched using this technology will fail. Learning, experience, and correction, and integrating AI in medical practices, will be an absolute prerequisite if AI applications are to function efficiently. This is something Robert Wachter (2015) points out in his book, *The Digital Doctor*.

When AI becomes fully integrated within most areas and levels of healthcare, we will most probably have to reformulate many of the basic notions we have about healthcare. The very core of medical practice is medical expertise and competence. In this context, this is precisely where AI will make an impact due to the development of learning and evolutionary algorithms. In other words, in the future we will most probably see a fusion of traditional medical practices and AI applications (Al-Turmjan et al., 2022; Bohr & Memarzadeh, 2020).

Expertise is the very basis for the development of AI in the healthcare sector. This may challenge the perceptions of doctors and specialist nurses when it becomes apparent that the new technological applications will have expertise that is equivalent to theirs. This may result in a situation where opposition to the new technology emerges, because it will challenge the competencies of doctors, nurses, and other health professionals. An intelligent robot that has the ability to transform competence into medical care will, with a great degree of certainty, meet a lot of resistance from the established health professions. If intelligent robots are able to make safer and better decisions than doctors and nurses, then opposition to the development of this technology will most probably occur in many quarters, and for various reasons.

We can conclude this introduction by pointing out that although the use of AI in the healthcare sector will create many new opportunities, it will also, of historical necessity, result in resistance to the technology, and create new problems that will have to be tackled.

Narratives

Case letter 1: AI in medical practice

The field of medicine is utilizing AI, robotics, and intelligent "informats" to a great extent. Intelligent informats are intelligent robots that are connected to a global network of similar robots. In the field of medicine, this may concern specific competence areas, such as heart surgery, cancer treatment, and so on. The knowledge that is generated at one place in the network can be immediately utilized at other places in the network.

This development within the healthcare sector is being driven by rising costs over the last ten years. Moreover, it has become increasingly difficult to get hold of the various types of expertise that are in demand (Topol, 2019: 44–56). These two factors have pushed forward technological innovations in the healthcare sector. The new technology has the potential to increase productivity, and reduce labour costs, while increasing automation processes within the healthcare sector.

Computers have been used for many years in the medical profession, such as in the analysis and storage of medical data (Sidey-Gibbons & Sidey-Gibbons, 2019: 1–18). Against this background, the further development of AI and intelligent algorithms will offer new possibilities regarding medical examinations and diagnoses. AI applications can be especially useful in identifying patterns in medical data that are beyond human ability.[2] This development will improve the quality of medical examinations, diagnoses, treatments, and prognoses. In turn, this will facilitate the improved performance of doctors, while also reducing the pressure of work. It can be envisioned that this will also lead to quality improvement in patient care.

AI diagnoses have a major advantage in relation to diagnoses carried out by physicians, due to the ability of AI to predict the development of patterns based on medical data found in various samples; this will represent a major advancement in medical practices when AI is adopted within most medical areas. These medical samples can be obtained using a combination of different measurements. It is precisely this possibility to predict that makes the application of AI in medical practice efficient, more productive, and safer for the individual patient.

Doctors and other healthcare professionals working in hospitals will not necessarily need to acquire special expertise in machine learning, intelligent algorithms, deep learning, evolutionary algorithms, etc. The technologists who research, design, test, and develop AI healthcare applications will have special expertise within these fields. On the other hand, it will be an advantage if hospitals employ technical operators who can maintain and further develop the various AI applications.

AI methods can be especially useful in the prediction and diagnosis of diseases, even when based on relatively small inputs. It is in this context that AI can prove to be more efficient than diagnoses carried out by physicians without the help of AI. AI applications can recognize in a microsecond, the development course of a disease, and make decisions regarding optimal treatment. It is of course conceivable that AI applications can make mistakes in the same way physicians can make mistakes when analysing medical data. However, when using learning algorithms, AI applications are able to learn from errors, in order to make future analyses safer. Of course, physicians can also learn from their mistakes, but AI applications are able to do this more rapidly and efficiently than humans. It is such improvements in the analysis of medical data that represent an important innovation in AI healthcare. Deep learning is the new aspect here, although deep learning has been used to advantage in many other contexts, such as in the design of chess computers.[3] Deep learning within the medical field is increasing the quality, speed, and possibility of making better diagnoses and providing improved forecasts for future treatment. In this way, it can be said that AI applications will be able to greatly improve medical practices in the healthcare sector.

Case letter 2: AI history – a brief introduction

The field of AI research was established as early as the 1950s. At this early stage, AI involved interpreting and assessing data, learning from the data, and changing search behaviour on the basis of the data that were analysed (Simon, 2019). The field of research did not make many significant advances regarding practical applications in the first 50 years of its existence (Ashby, 1970; 1981; Simon, 1965).

The British mathematician, Alan Turing, can possibly be said to be the first person to work with AI for a practical purpose. During the Second World War, he developed an electromechanical machine for breaking the German codes that were encrypted by the Enigma machine. He wrote the groundbreaking article, "Computing Machinery and Intelligence," that was published in 1950.[4]

By the mid-1960s, AI research in the United States was heavily funded by the Department of Defense. Initial work included using AI as a tool to analyse large amounts of data. (Russel & Norvig, 2016). To a large extent, this work was done by information theorists and cyberneticists who tested various forms of steering and control functions using AI (Ashby, 1981). The first scientific work on AI was written by McCullough and Pitts (1943), which focused on their design for Turing-complete "artificial neurons"; an artificial neuron is a connection point in an artificial neural network.[5]

AI research beyond the 1950s and 1960s attempted to find symbolic representations of the external world in order to understand and interpret changes in external data. From this research grew a preoccupation with heuristic processes, where Pareto's 80/20 rule became important. This research resulted in a greater preoccupation with using AI in machines for learning where the American psychologist, Rosenblatt, was central.[6] These two fields, involving symbolic representations and machines capable of learning developed towards "connectionism" and neural network research.[7] "Connectionism," which belongs to the field of cybernetics, is an approach to the study of human mental processes and cognition that uses mathematical models, or more specifically, artificial neural networks.[8] From this point on, AI became more and more oriented towards the field of mathematics and statistics, as a basis for synthetic intelligence. Up until the late 1980s and the early 1990s, AI became a field of research that attempted to solve current problems for various areas of application. Large amounts of data connected to machine learning were developed to solve the challenges in various fields and areas, such as chess-playing machines, banking, investments, and so on. With new developments in algorithm research at the beginning of the 2000s, and the development of faster and more powerful computers, it can be said that AI was having a new renaissance.

Around 2012–2015, AI experienced a new boom, when "deep learning" became a new technology that was used to develop various areas of application for AI.[9] Neural networks gained new relevance with the new technology related to "deep learning." It is, among other things, based on these developments that new language models came into use, such as ChatGPT, an AI-powered language model (November 2022).[10] ChatGPT received much attention in 2023, and several research communities produced articles questioning the direction and purpose of future AI development; many of these articles warned about AI development getting completely out of control.

The future development of AI will probably focus on natural language processing and the collection and analysis of large amounts of data, where patterns and pattern recognition appear to be an important field of research. Among other things, this will be of interest to political actors, governments, and the military. For example, the Chinese authorities have developed surveillance programmes for facial recognition with the aim of social behaviour control. Moreover, AI is now being used in a broad range of weapon systems, such as guided missiles, and land, air, and sea drones. It is also possible that the future will see a greater emphasis on the development of social and emotional intelligence in the next generations of AI.

Case letter 3: AI in medicine – a brief historical introduction

Although AI has a general history dating back to the 1950s, it was first with the introduction of deep-learning technology around 2020 that AI began to make a major impact in the medical field (Porter & Teisberg, 2006). It became possible to utilize the new AI learning algorithms to tackle the increasing complexity in the healthcare sector. This applied to both risk assessments and for diagnostic purposes.

However, it can also be argued that AI was used in medical development as early as the 1980s, and even before this. Though, this mainly concerned information handling, rather than the medical AI applications that are used today. Nevertheless, the development of medical expert systems, that utilized artificial intelligence, made it possible to make predictions and treatment recommendations, similar to those carried out by medical experts. In other words, some of these expert systems could also mimic human decision-making (Britnell, 2019). DENDRAL, an early expert system, developed in 1965, was one such analysis expert system, that could be used for effective decision-making. The MYCIN computer-based consultation system was developed in the 1970s, followed in the 1980s by CADUCEUS, another medical expert system.[11] However, these early expert systems never quite managed to live up to the high expectations of medical professionals, eventually resulting in a loss of interest for further development (Bohr & Memarzadeh, 2020). It was first around the 2000s, with the introduction of various innovations in AI algorithms and deep-learning applications, that decision-support systems in the healthcare sector again received renewed interest (Al-Turmjan et al., 2022). The machine learning systems that were developed for other contexts also captured interest in the healthcare sector (Reddy, 2021: 1–14). A technique that received a lot of attention was image diagnostics for various medical fields, such as analysis of X-rays and gastroenterology (Mahajan, 2021: 413).

It is on the basis of the practical application of AI within various medical fields, from the 2000s onwards, that AI first became functional in medical practices. It was especially research related to deep learning, algorithms, hardware, and not least technological infrastructure such as 5G networks, that AI in healthcare gained momentum. However, it was the development of the technology related to neural networks, which created interest in the practical applications of AI in the healthcare sector.[12] An important point was that the complexity of the medical problems could find a high degree of sufficient complexity in the technology being used, so that relevant problems could be solved. It may be argued that it was when the emerging new technology allowed the requisite variety of skills (Ashby, 1961; 1970; 1981) to be brought to bear to tackle medical problems that the medical profession was able to apply and further develop this technology.

From this point on, the applications of AI in medical practice have greatly increased. It is especially within the following areas where AI applications have been utilized, or are in the process of developing new methods (Mahajan, 2021: 324–465):

- Prevention healthcare.
- Nutrition.
- Radiology.
- Pathology.
- Surgery.

- Anaesthesiology.
- Psychiatry.
- Cardiology.
- Pharmacy.
- Dermatology.
- Dentistry.
- Orthopaedics.
- Ophthalmology.
- Critical Care Medicine.
- Emergency Medicine.
- Endocrinology.
- Gastroenterology.
- Haematology.
- Infectious Diseases.
- Primary Care.
- Nephrology.
- Neurology and Neurosurgery.
- Obstetrics and Gynaecology.
- Oncology.
- Paediatrics.
- Pulmonology.
- Rheumatology.
- Nursing.
- Physical Therapy.
- Veterinary Medicine.
- Healthcare Administration.

This brief historical introduction and the description of the newer areas of application for AI in healthcare indicate that there is a large potential for the future use of AI in healthcare.

Description regarding the potential uses of AI in healthcare

As shown in the case letters, there are many opportunities that open up for the future use of AI in the healthcare sector. We will limit our discussion here to five areas: "mobile healthcare", the productivity of healthcare workers, a greater focus on healthcare workers, life expectancy, a qualitative improvement of people's lives, and the importance of the view that humans are underrated, despite the advancements in new technology.

"Mobile healthcare"

Mobile health is more complex than just ordering the delivery of online health services, in the same way that we might order a book from Amazon online. One of the reasons for this is that people trust a face-to-face consultation with a doctor or nurse more than they might trust an online medical consultation. However, it may be imagined that attitudes will change when AI-driven services have become more "intelligent", and when a "digital doctor" is only a keystroke away (Watcher, 2015; Al-Turmjan et al., 2022).

It is very probable that we will witness disruptive innovations in the future healthcare industry that will impact both healthcare systems, patients, and users (Billington, 2020; Hamel, 2007; 2008; 2012). In other words, changes will most probably occur on many levels and in various professional areas. In this context, mobile health will become a topical issue. The relationships between health professionals and patients will change, because patients will become more used to dealing with intelligent care robots, and the health professions will be more skilled at helping patients via digital networks. Of course, there will still be a need for face-to-face medical consultations. The further development of mobile healthcare will reduce costs, free up resources, and reduce the pressure of work for health professionals making it possible for them to devote more time to patients who have a greater need for personal medical attention. Thus, it can be argued that the development of mobile healthcare will result in the availability of more hands-on medical professionals rather than less.

The productivity of healthcare workers (knowledge workers)

In P.F. Drucker's renowned article, "Knowledge worker productivity: The biggest challenge," he asked the question: How can we increase the productivity of knowledge workers? (Drucker, 1999; 1999a; Wong, 2013).

Drucker suggested that there are six major factors that determine knowledge worker productivity, these are:

1. Task definition: "What is the task?"
2. Productivity of the knowledge worker is dependent not only on quantity but also on quality.
3. Continuing innovation processes are important for the work and the task.
4. The knowledge worker should be viewed as an "asset" rather than a "cost."
5. Autonomy: The knowledge workers are responsible for their own productivity; i.e., they need to manage themselves.
6. Continuous learning: Knowledge work demands a continuous upgrading of skills.

The first factor regarding knowledge worker productivity demands that we ask the question: "What is the task?" In other words, what is the system designed to do? It is what the system is designed to do that should be allocated resources. If it is shown that much of the time and resources go to tasks other than what the system is designed to do, then these tasks need to be eliminated or delegated to others than the health professionals in order to increase focus on those areas that should be given priority. It is in this context that AI and digital solutions can provide an opportunity to enable healthcare workers to focus on their core tasks, i.e., what the system is designed to do.

The second factor that Drucker identified as important to knowledge worker productivity concerned the fact that productivity of the knowledge worker is dependent not only on quantity but also on quality. The knowledge worker should have a clear idea about how his/her productivity is being measured. For example, this may concern certain quality criteria or the time spent on a work activity. In other words, the knowledge worker needs to know what is expected of him/her with regard to work tasks. As a general rule, this is often resolved through personnel discussions between the worker and the team leader.

The third factor was related to innovation processes. The healthcare worker or team should be given the time and resources to participate in the development of innovations within their own work area. It may be imagined that innovation processes could also be related to the productivity orientation in the second factor above. In this context, the use of AI in the healthcare sector will be able to facilitate innovation orientation, because it will then be easier to obtain information about important current problems that can be solved using innovative solutions.

The fourth factor that Drucker found to be important to knowledge worker productivity was that the knowledge worker should be viewed as an "asset" rather than a "cost." In practical terms, this could mean that knowledge workers who receive positive feedback from their leaders perform better. This factor can be related to Asplund's Motivation Theory, which states that "people are motivated by social responses" (Asplund, 1970; 2010). This is a relatively simple method that leaders can use to increase the productivity of healthcare workers.

The fifth factor Drucker pointed out concerns "autonomy." Knowledge workers are responsible for their own productivity; i.e., they need to manage themselves. In practice, this means that the healthcare workers should have the freedom to organize their own work so that this will give the best results. In this context, it may be imagined that AI can be used as a support function when healthcare workers are organizing their work schedules.

The sixth factor indicated by Drucker was "continuous learning." It was found that when knowledge workers were able to continuously upgrade their skills this led to increased performance. This sixth factor is extremely important at a time when rapid changes are occurring in the development and application of new technology.

However, it is the interaction between these six factors that gave the best performance improvements, not that a leader focuses on one or some of the six factors. It is by focusing on all six factors, together with the new opportunities created by the development of AI, that offers the greatest potential for productivity gains in the healthcare sector.

A focus on healthcare workers

It is not the intention of the conceptual model (Figure 3.1) that the increased productivity of healthcare workers should worsen their working environment. On the contrary, the introduction of new technological applications may increase

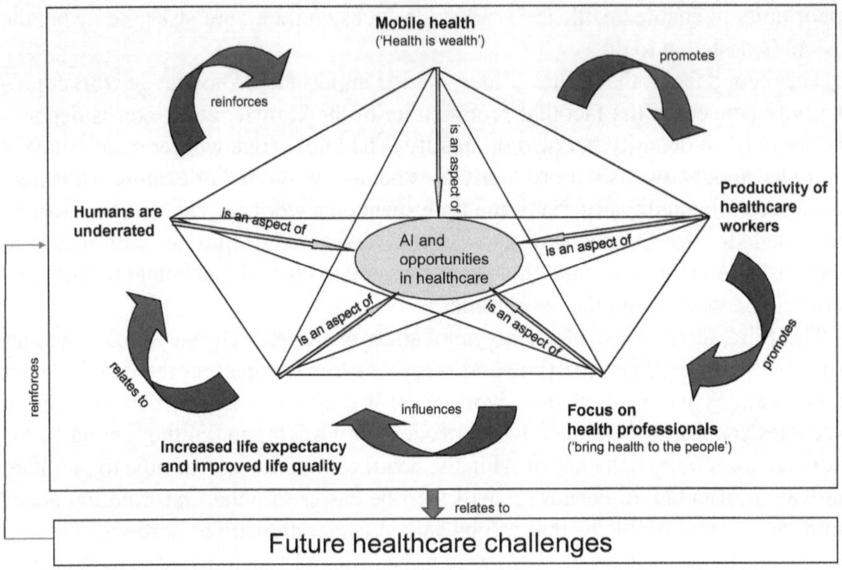

Figure 3.1 Aspects of AI and opportunities in the healthcare sector: A conceptual model.

productivity, but it will also lessen the burden of physically and mentally demanding activities and increase the quality of work, resulting in an improved working environment. The rationale is that AI applications will be able to reduce the burden of physically and mentally demanding work activities, and thus reduce work injuries and ailments. For instance, it has been shown that AI has improved the working environment of employees in the pharmacy industry (Flynn, 2019), and also reduced the pressure of work for the leaders of health institutions (Motulsky et al., 2021: 91–101). As we have shown in the introduction to this chapter, machine learning applications have facilitated the interests of health professionals in their working environment. Also in Chapter 2, regarding the lack of hands-on healthcare personnel, AI applications will give healthcare workers more time to focus on their core activities. Therefore, the introduction of new AI technology will be able to promote the interests of healthcare professionals so they can perform their work in a more effective and satisfactory manner.

The positive attitudes regarding the increased use of AI in healthcare are also related to the more efficient collection of data, which can improve communication with patients in their home situation. This will ease the pressure of work for healthcare workers and may improve the quality of healthcare services (Flynn, 2019: 622–627). The increased use of AI will enable the leadership of healthcare systems to collect large amounts of data, which can then be used to communicate information with various healthcare professionals. This will improve communication, providing a better basis for making decisions, and thus promote the quality of healthcare work.

AI and robotics are being increasingly used in healthcare, transforming clinical practices, and taking over many healthcare tasks. While there are countless benefits of using robots in healthcare, there is also the likelihood of errors and failures. But the same could also be said about healthcare professionals. However, it is probable that the increased use of AI and robotics in healthcare will lead to less rather than more errors. It is also probable that the use of AI and robotics will enable a greater focus on the core activities of healthcare professionals, freeing up resources and improving working conditions. In other words, the increased use of AI and robotics will open up new opportunities for healthcare professionals, but we should also keep in mind the fact that robotics in healthcare can also have some negative impacts.

Life expectancy and a qualitative improvement of people's lives

The further development of AI and robotics in healthcare will most probably lead to an improved quality of life, and increased lifespan. Since 1900, life expectancy has greatly increased and will further increase with the introduction of new technology (Wood, 2020). However, this will also result in new challenges, regarding an ageing global population. In this context, the new technology will also be able to help elderly people take care of themselves at home for longer than was the case before, and with greater safety. The elderly will also have the opportunity to work longer by using AI in various ways. The fact that the elderly will be able to manage themselves at home to a greater extent than before by using AI applications will also ease the pressure of the work of health professionals, as discussed in the previous section. In this way, we can envision an organization of the health services that enables people to receive medical help in their homes, or in the community where they live. In other words, the possibility of "bringing health to the people" in the communities where they live. Of course, in this context we are not only talking about elderly care, but also other groups of people who have a need of health services; they would also be able to live qualitatively better lives if the health services are brought to them, than if, e.g., they have to travel relatively long distances to receive medical help. In other words, if the above assumptions are correct, then the future use of AI in healthcare will provide great benefits for people and society in the form of better quality of life and increased life expectancy.

Humans are underrated

AI means different things to different people. However, what we can say with certainty is that despite the impact of AI on people's lives, human competences, i.e., their knowledge, skills and attitudes, will still be crucial for helping people in need. In this context, we can say that "humans are underrated," or rather, their competences are underrated. No matter how much productivity increases with the increased use of artificial intelligence in healthcare, there will always be a need for people who can show empathy, i.e., people who have the ability to understand and share the feelings of others. In other words, although the use of AI can improve the quality of health services, such as improved diagnoses and treatment, and consequently improve and increase people's quality of life and lifespan, there will still be a need for "caring hands," i.e., hands-on health professionals who can provide that warm touch (Britnell, 2019; Mahajan, 2021).

Sophisticated AI technology can learn from its own mistakes. For example, chess programmes that are based on a learning algorithm, and then programmed with the rules of the chess game, have been able to find the best moves by playing against itself in simulated games, and thus able to beat the best chess players in the world. In other words, no one doubts that intelligent computer programs are logical, but can AI understand people's irrational thinking?

Our childhood experiences, our language, and our experiences in adult life all contribute to personality development. People with similar and dissimilar backgrounds will communicate with each other in a way that can be said to be uniquely human. In other words, it might be said that AI will never be able to replicate this type of human communication that is built on people's life histories. Of course, it may be argued that it will be possible to program a computer with certain skills that mimic childhood and adult experiences, but there will be something else, something alien, where empathy and reciprocity are lacking. It may be possible to develop intelligent robots so that they can reflect with us on future possibilities, taking into account childhood experiences that can influence our behaviour in the here and now. It is also possible that these robots can change their behaviour as a result of such reflection. On the other hand, it will never be possible for AI and robotics to replicate human shared experience, i.e., the type of communication that occurs when two people with similar backgrounds and assumptions converse with each other. In other words, it is this meeting between people that AI in the healthcare sector will always fall short. The practical clinical use of AI can, and will very likely in the future, improve many of the processes in the healthcare sector, resulting in higher productivity and improved quality. On the other hand, there are skills these robots will never be able to master, and these are the skills of a nurse with "caring hands," and a "clinical gaze," i.e., her/his ability to communicate with the patient, and focus and be aware of a patient's needs, life phenomena, and their experiences of hope, suffering, and anxiety.

Based on the above introduction, narratives and description, we have developed a conceptual model related to AI and opportunities in the healthcare sector.

Narratives

Case letter 4: Surgical robots – advantages

The future of surgery is likely to include AI robots that can function independently. AI-enabled navigation systems put wheelchair users in control enabling the navigation of doorways and unexpected obstacles, and also enabling them to find the best routes to their destinations, such as service centres in their local environment.

Many surgical operations that cannot be performed today, due to a lack of expertise, may in the near future be performed by surgical robots. The prerequisite for this to be possible is that the information structure (info-structure) is developed and reliable. It is in this context that 5G and 6G networks are important to enable the optional functioning of surgical robots. Throughout this book we have stressed that it takes a long time before new technology is fully developed and implemented in a society. AI research began as early as the 1940s and 1950s, though, the breakthrough of AI in healthcare first became more visible around 2020. However, surgical robots have a long history in medical care stretching back several decades to the 1980s.

The first records of robotic surgery date back to 1985 (Shah et al., 2014). It is important to be aware of the history of surgical robots, so that one has an overview of what a surgical robot can do, and what it cannot do. It is possible that new types of surgical robots will be developed in the future that will be able to perform operations independently, but this is not the case today. In today's context, robotic-assisted surgery functions as a supportive tool for the surgeon, enabling him/her to perform more precise surgery.

In recent years, robotic cardiac surgery has made many advances, using tiny instruments and robot-controlled tools (Sridhar et al. 2017). It is probable that this technology will be further developed with the future development of 6G networks. In such a context, AI surgical robots in the future will probably become an integrated component of telemedicine, i.e., enabling the provision of remote medical help to people in rural and outlying areas who previously have not had access to this type of medical help.

In the future, robotic surgery will become more advanced and effective, and play a major role in medical practice (Al-Turmjan et al., 2022). Robotic surgery will offer numerous benefits for most patients, including more precise and accurate operations, and better visualization of the surgical area. The technology will also make it possible for the surgeon to carry out the operation reducing the extent of incisions, and thus bleeding and infections. In addition, as mentioned above, technology will be an important component in telemedicine, so that it will be possible to perform operations remotely.

The future possibilities of surgical robots and surgically assisted robotics in healthcare will be wide-ranging. This assumption is especially important at a time when there is a lack of "caring hands" in the healthcare sector. The paradox is, as we have pointed out earlier, that the lack of "caring hands" promotes the use of AI-related technology, which in turn increases automation and productivity, and thus frees up more "caring hands."

Although it is 40 years since the first surgical robotics were used in surgical procedures, it is only in recent years that it has become an invaluable tool in most major surgical operations. However, although surgical robotics is being increasingly used, it is still the surgeon who is responsible for the actual surgical operation. The advantage of using robotic-assisted surgery is that it enables the surgeon to perform operations with greater precision and accuracy.

There has also been an increasing use of surgical robots in cancer operations, e.g., because the visual feedback system provides greater opportunity for the surgeon to perform the best possible surgical intervention (Boyraz et al., 2019: 431–450).

The development we have seen from the 1980s up until 2024 shows us that the future possibilities for the use of AI and intelligent robots in the healthcare sector are almost inexhaustible. It is possibly in the field of surgical robotics that the new technology will make its greatest impact in the healthcare sector.

Case letter 5: Surgical robots – disadvantages

With a greater use of surgical robotics, surgeons will also need to acquire surgical robotics skills. In other words, skilled surgeons may face problems and challenges if they do not acquire these skills, which will be needed to use the new surgical robotics tools. The new skills we are referring to here are cutting-edge expertise in AI in general, and specific skills related to using surgical robotics tools. Acquiring new skills in AI and surgical robotics may prove to be problematic for some surgeons, who are used to being the sole authority and "king" in the operating theatre. It is also possible that new professions will emerge, such as technicians who have expertise in using surgical robotics tools. In other words, the staffing of operating theatres in the future may be organized in a different way than it is today.

Another possible disadvantage of robot-assisted surgery is related to trust. That is, do people trust robot-assisted surgery? In this context, there are two crucial factors. If the surgical robotics equipment does not depend on an external network to function optimally, then trust in the technology will depend on the expertise of the surgeon, or the staff in the operating theatre who have expertise in using robotics tools. In such a situation, it will be less difficult for patients to have trust in the technology, than if the surgical robotics is dependent on an external network to function properly. If there is increased complexity, then trust in robot-assisted surgery may face challenges. The surgical robotics tools may function optimally, but the external network may not function one-hundred per cent, resulting in a loss of confidence in the robotics technology.

The description above regarding malfunctioning surgical robotics equipment is not just taken out of thin air. A retrospective study of 14 years (from 2000 to 2013), regarding the adverse events in robotic surgery, conducted in the United States, reported 144 deaths and 1,391 patient injuries. The study also showed that the deaths and injuries had remained relatively constant throughout the 14 years.[13] The study also showed that robotics surgery used within gynaecology and urology, where robots are extensively used, had lower numbers of injuries and deaths than more complex surgeries. The study also proposes that understanding the causes of adverse events when using robot-assisted surgery will help improve operational practices to avoid malfunctioning in the future.

Many of the negative effects of using robotic surgery, resulting in deaths and injuries, were due to malfunctioning equipment during surgical procedures. In this context, the acquisition of new skills mentioned above may prove beneficial; i.e., new professions that are technologically competent in using robotics equipment. This would most probably reduce the number of deaths and injuries.

By 2024, and beyond, it can be expected that surgical robotics will have improved considerably in relation to the period of the study mentioned above (2000–2013). The study was conducted at a time when surgical robotics was at an early stage of technological development. It may also be envisioned that robot-assisted surgery will become more complex in the future, and will most probably demand new skills and possibly new professions. In other words, it is most probable that a qualitatively new profession will become part of surgical teams. These professionals will have expertise in the use of artificial intelligence and the high-tech tools used in surgical operations.

Analysis related to AI, and opportunities in the healthcare sector

Artificial intelligence (AI) provides the medical profession with a whole new toolbox that opens up many opportunities regarding the analysis of medical data, amongst other things. Over time, the costs of applying this technology will fall due to economies of scale. This has been shown historically in many economic areas (Frey, 2019; 2020; Baumol, 2012). When costs fall and productivity increases, investors show greater interest. This development is also evident regarding the use of artificial intelligence in healthcare systems (Bohr & Memarzadeh, 2020).

As we move into the Fourth Industrial Revolution, it is expected that the utilization of AI and robotics will spread quickly throughout the economy. In contrast, the technology of previous industrial revolutions took a long time, often a very long time, before it became an essential part of everyday life for most people (Frey, 2019). It is also possible, as described earlier, that the same will apply to the development of artificial intelligence. However, it might also be said that the development of artificial intelligence has reached a "tipping point," an exponential rate of development, and has the potential to revolutionize many different industries; not least, the healthcare industry, where AI and robotics are being increasingly utilized (Britnell, 2019; Mahajan, 2021).

The development of artificial intelligence (AI) over the last 70 years has resulted in the situation we find ourselves in today, where artificial intelligence can "think" like humans, at least with regard to logical thinking and reasoning. This development is also creating resistance to technology. When AI machine learning was developed to design a computing programme that could play games such as chess on a human level, then there were few who objected. On the other hand, when AI is utilized to generate medical decisions when we are lying on the surgeon's operating table, this seems a bit frightening. It is also frightening that this technology is being increasingly used in military decision-making processes and in the development of gene-edited plants, and so on (Carey, 2019). This is also why many people oppose the unregulated development of the technology and have sent letters to political decision-makers asking for a reduction in the speed at which this technology is being developed. In this book, we have mentioned several such objections to the development of AI. However, as of today, there is still no consensus on how we want to develop the technology.

Artificial intelligence (AI) is a powerful tool for medical data collection, storage, analysis and retrieval, for use in clinical research studies, diagnoses, and for making health policy decisions. However, there are many examples of how such processes have not always functioned according to expectations. On the other hand, the potential of applying AI in paediatric medicine to diagnose and treat childhood diseases will no doubt reduce scepticism, regarding the future development of the technology.

Up until today, AI applications have been mainly used for administrative tasks within healthcare, and as a tool for assisting with diagnosis and the prediction of disease outcomes. In the future, it is probable that AI will be used in the field of mental health, such as creating personalized treatments for mental health conditions. It is also probable that AI analysis will be increasingly used to enable the screening and analysis of various genetic diseases.[14]

It is especially the potential of AI to assist in improving the quality of healthcare that will be focused on in the future. The demand for increasing the quality of healthcare is increasing around the world (Sqalli et al., 2021: 41–51). For instance, AI applications can assist medical personnel to make more accurate diagnoses and predict how patients may react to therapies. This will enable improved treatment plans and reduce medical errors. It is also probable that AI can be increasingly used in elderly healthcare by enabling personalized monitoring and care.

AI and Big Data are being increasingly used to conduct analyses in healthcare (Saxena et al., 2021; Carou et al., 2022). These AI analyses can identify patterns and relationships in the data in a qualitatively better way than medical personnel with no access to AI. These patterns can then be used at a policy level, but also for clinical research, in order to find improved treatment options for various illnesses. As mentioned above, AI can be used to improve medical diagnosis, treatment, and healthcare delivery. Rapid analysis of health data, more precise diagnoses and timely interventions all contribute to improving the quality of healthcare. There are many examples here. For instance, AI can be used to carry out gastrointestinal cancer examinations, image analysis of X-rays, and many other diagnostic processes, where AI can detect abnormalities and pattern changes in the data at an earlier stage than the human eye. This can result in patients receiving earlier treatment, and thus a greater probability of a better outcome, than without this technology.[15]

Although this technology is important for the outcome of treatment, and the patient's well-being before, during, and after a medical intervention, the interaction between the patient and medical personnel is decisive for the overall quality of treatment and care.[16]

The development regarding increased demand for healthcare, on the one hand, and technological progress within AI in healthcare, on the other hand, has initially led to many health systems introducing digitalization processes in management systems, in addition to using AI tools for diagnosis, analysis, and treatment. As these systems are continually developed and become easier to operate, they will increase technology's intervention in various decision-making processes. This assumption is based on historical analogies with the development and application of new technologies.[17]

There is thus a trend of increasing the use of AI in various parts and levels of the healthcare system on the one hand. On the other hand, it is precisely this increasing use of AI in the healthcare sector that paradoxically leads to an increase in the interaction between medical personnel and patients. The reasons for this have been explained in several places in this book so far. The application of AI in the healthcare sector is increasing the automation of work processes, resulting in increased productivity, and increased quality in analyses, diagnoses, and treatment. This will also lead to an increase in the use of frontline medical personnel.

In order to envision possible future scenarios in healthcare, we will conduct a small thought experiment. In the future, if AI-driven medical robots are distributed in a network enabled by the development of the future 6G network, this will enable the provision of remote healthcare services to people in rural and remote districts. In other words, it will be possible for people in rural and remote districts to hire these medical robots for various medical examinations and treatments. These peripheral areas may be within industrialized countries, but also in underdeveloped regions of the world. In this way, medical robots could provide healthcare services, "medical robots for hire," to those areas of the world where healthcare services are poor.

Narratives related to AI and opportunities in the healthcare sector

Case letter 6: Longevity and a qualitatively better life

Without doubt AI will become important for determining the quality of life of the elderly (Villaronga & Drukarch, 2022). Longevity is not the only consideration here, we are also interested in AI's potential to improve older people's quality of life. As the demographic prospect of an increasingly elderly population becomes a reality we will see a growth in research and investment in technology to improve older people's well-being. Already we see how researchers are focusing on biological markers that can assist with early disease diagnosis and treatment and other interventions designed to prevent health issues from having a negative impact on quality of life (Woods, 2020: 8). Currently much research is being conducted into AI, algorithms, and ageing.[18] This research has assisted in the development of causal models that allow the application of AI to identify disease progression in individual cases, and suggest ways of preserving individuals' quality of life through the choice and timing of medical interventions. In fact, the most recent research suggests that AI could be used to develop customized drugs for individual patients.[19] Similarly, AI could be used to conduct analyses in a much larger, or Big Data, context, as well as for analysing an individual's biological processes, so that medicines can be delivered according to a customized schedule.

A few basic statistics illustrate the importance of conducting research into AI and ageing. In 2060, in the United States alone, 98 million people will be aged 65 or over. In 2040, around 14.6 million Americans will be aged 85 or over.[20] These figures suggest a likely huge demand for research and investment in the coming years. The law of large numbers alone suggests that researchers' focus on the elderly will only increase.

As people age, their risk of disease and chronic conditions increases. For this reason, demand for medical services – both for "first line competence" and for technological solutions – will only increase in the years to 2060. In 2018, a study from the United States showed that 52 per cent of Americans aged over 85 had one chronic condition, while 26 per cent had multiple chronic conditions. In addition,

34 per cent were living with a disability, such as impaired vision, hearing loss, or poor mobility.[21] These figures suggest that research into this population group is likely to increase in the future, as will efforts to provide technological solutions. Older people are not only affected by physical challenges but they may also be affected by cognitive disorders. These disorders could impair, e.g., the ability to drive or to continue some aspects of a professional practice. Perhaps the most serious and dreaded cognitive challenges are those associated with Alzheimer's disease, which affects memory as well as other faculties. Unless a cure is found for Alzheimer's, approximately 12.7 million people will be affected by the disease in 2050 in the United States alone.[22]

In the future, AI-driven technology will be able to help us meet the needs of our ageing population. The following description mentions some of the ways we will be able to do this:

1. Smart home technologies: Most seniors want to live in their homes as long as possible. Therefore, various intelligent technological solutions will be in demand in the future. These technologies can be used for cleaning, ordering food, monitoring, cooking technologies, smart lighting systems, automatic coffee machines, voice activation of various functions, nightly monitoring of movement and physical condition, medication-management technologies, direct link to healthcare agencies, etc.
2. Portable patient monitors: For instance, Apple-watch apps that can support clients and clinicians in relation to a client's medical condition, and in relation to various aspects of health including heart and circulatory health, mobility, activity, medication, and so on.
3. "Virtual reality": Here you can imagine that the elderly have direct video contact with family, friends, and others, so that they can see and communicate in real time with others. In this way, for the elderly who live on their own, the feeling of loneliness will be reduced (Sanchez-Vives et al., 2005: 332–339).
4. Intelligent robots: Regarding the use of artificial intelligence (AI) and robotics to help the care of the elderly, it is only our imaginations that limit the possibilities. For instance, artificial intelligence (AI) and robotics can help the elderly who are living with physical and mental disabilities in relation to medical support, improving accessibility and mobility, and improving social connections (Allaban et al., 2020; Pu et al., 2019).

Theoretical reflections related to AI and opportunities in the healthcare sector

In the following, we will examine two variables that seem to be decisive regarding the scope of opportunities for the use of AI in healthcare. These two variables are the degree of focus on mobile health, and the degree of focus on the performance of healthcare workers (Househ et al., 2021).

"Mobile health," abbreviated as mHealth, is a term used for the practice of medicine and healthcare supported by mobile devices, such as mobile phones, tablet computers, and so on. The mHealth field is a sub-segment of eHealth, i.e., the use of information and communication technology (ICT) in health services. Although mHealth does not utilize AI applications to any great extent, it may be assumed this is a development that will occur in the future. In 2019, seven mHealth applications were reported to be in use[23]:

1. Education and Awareness.
2. Helpline.
3. Diagnostic and Treatment Support.
4. Communication and Training for Healthcare Workers.
5. Disease and Epidemic Outbreak Tracking.
6. Remote Monitoring.
7. Remote Data Collection.

With the further development of AI and robotics, as well as the further development of what we term here as "intelligent informats,"[24] it will be possible to expand mHealth with the help of this new technology. The new practical applications within mHealth will increase opportunities within the healthcare sector. By applying AI, the gap between the user of mHealth and the healthcare system will be reduced considerably. When a healthcare worker is in face-to-face contact with a patient, the quality of the communication and consultation can be improved when the healthcare worker has access to an intelligent informat. Patients will also be able to independently access an intelligent informat, in order to inquire about a medical condition, and a possible diagnosis and treatment without having to contact a healthcare worker. Both of these two examples will very likely increase the productivity of healthcare workers.

By integrating AI into mHealth, it will be possible to personalize the services to users in a qualitatively better way than is the case today. The rationale is that AI can obtain an overview of a user's needs, which would be too complex without the help of such technology. The integration of AI and mHealth can also make it possible to both monitor and medicate a patient in their home situation. For example, the monitoring of heartbeat, pulse rate, calorie intake, etc. In addition to a more personalized service, it will be possible to achieve better preventive health measures by using AI-integrated solutions in mHealth. When the healthcare systems, by using this technology, can monitor the physical and mental health of a patient, the health worker's productivity will increase greatly. This will occur because more healthcare personnel will be available where they are most needed, when healthcare providers can care for patients without making in-person home visits.

On the basis of the above narratives, description, and theoretical reflection, we have developed four propositions for the relationship between mobile health and the performance of healthcare workers.

Proposition 1: The greater the degree of focus on mobile health, and the greater the degree of focus on the performance of health workers, the greater the

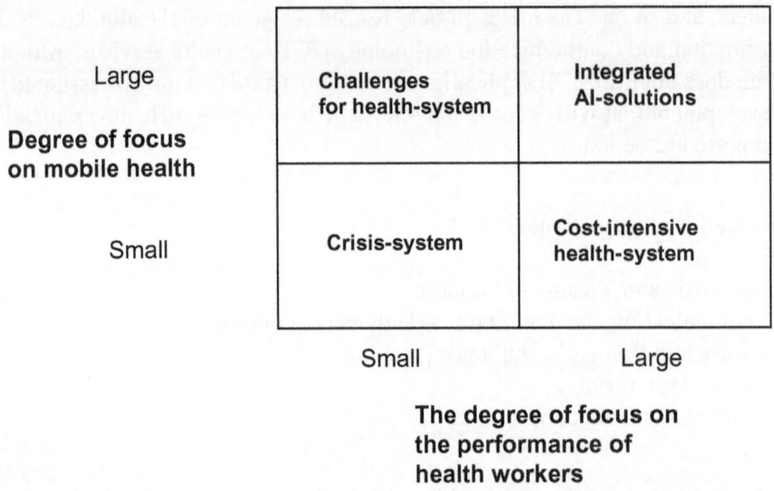

Figure 3.2 Integrated AI solutions: A typology.

likelihood that integrated AI solutions will be developed in the healthcare sector (Figure 3.2).

When healthcare workers can acquire training in the use of AI applications when using an mHealth system, this will lead to integrated AI solutions that will boost productivity. In addition, healthcare workers will be able to develop a greater degree of autonomy, and self-management, and use the time that becomes available for other purposes, such as innovation development (Drucker, 1999; 1999a).

Proposition 2: The greater the degree of focus on mobile health, and the less focus there is on the performance of healthcare workers, the greater the likelihood that the healthcare system will be faced with challenges.

The reasoning here is related to the fact that technology in itself can be positive in some contexts, but if a new technological development is not put in relation to the healthcare workers' productivity, then you can quickly end up with good technological solutions, but without necessarily increasing the competence of the individual healthcare worker. This can result in the healthcare system facing various challenges. One of these challenges is related to increasing costs, which we refer to in Proposition 3. Another challenge is related to the fact that if the technology is not compatible with the healthcare workers' level of competence, this can lead to solutions that do not result in the healthcare system functioning optimally.

Proposition 3: The smaller the degree of focus on mobile health, and the greater the degree of focus on the performance of the healthcare worker, the greater the likelihood that a cost-intensive system will be developed in the healthcare sector.

The reasoning is related to the fact that even if the performance of the health workers is increased, the relative costs will increase, even if the real costs fall. The point of this distinction is to show that competition between different health systems will always be a factor in a health market. If the relative costs in one health system increase, while the real costs in a competing health system decrease, then the probability is high that the system that manages to lower costs by combining an increased focus on both mobile health and the productivity of the health workers will be the superior system. The relative costs in the original system will therefore have a negative impact on this competitive situation.

Proposition 4: The less focus on mobile health, and the less focus on the performance of healthcare workers, the greater the likelihood that a crisis system will develop in the healthcare sector.

The reasoning here is simple. If you neither focus on mobile health nor on the productivity of the healthcare workers, you will be left behind in the competition, when there is a relatively free market for health services.

On the basis of the four propositions and the above theoretical reflection, we have developed a typology for opportunities that will exist when using AI in the healthcare sector related to the two variables we have reviewed.

Practical utility related to AI and opportunities in the healthcare sector

Throughout this book, we have argued that human factors are important in healthcare. On the other hand, we have also argued that AI, robotics, and intelligent informats are also important for making more "first line competence" available in the healthcare sector. Demographic developments, and especially the ageing population, mean there will be an increased number of elderly people who will need healthcare in the future. This will increase costs in the public and private sectors. It is also to get ahead of this development that we argue strongly for increased robotization and automation of work functions in healthcare, but also in the economy as a whole. In addition, such a development will most probably demand that the various health professions become more competent in using the new technology and learn new skills. It is also possible that new technological professions will emerge in the healthcare sector, due to the increased use of AI and robotics. Throughout this book, we have also argued strongly that AI, robotization, and automation will increase productivity. We are of the opinion that it is the increase in productivity that will to a great extent solve many of the challenges that the healthcare sector will face in the future.

The further development of AI in clinical practices will result in the technology being used to replace work functions that were previously carried out by health personnel. This applies to the field of surgery, nursing care, and the economic-administrative system. As AI takes over many functions within these areas, automation and productivity will increase, and more and more human resources will be available, so that the healthcare sector can focus more on what it is designed to do, namely provide various forms of help and care to those who need it, and thus improve patient care. These AI-related solutions are already being used, but will increase in scope in the future. It is this development that we have tried to make a contribution to in this chapter. We are of the opinion that it is precisely the paradox that automation makes more people redundant, which in turn provides more "first line competence" for the healthcare sector. In this way, it can be argued that "humans are underrated" in relation to the introduction of new technology. Our main argument in this chapter has been that there is a systemic connection between AI and "first line competence." It is precisely the "cold" technology that will provide more "first line competence" to those who need it.

In his book, *The Cost Disease: Why Computers Get Cheaper and Health Care Doesn't* (2012), Baumol pointed out several years ago that although digital technology was becoming more affordable, healthcare costs were nevertheless increasing. It is precisely this development we are also witnessing today. The rationale is largely related to demographic developments and the new opportunities that the new technology is creating in relation to new types of medical treatment. The demographic challenge concerns the ageing population and the increased costs regarding healthcare for the elderly. However, this problem can be solved in relation to what Baumol so rightly pointed out, that the technology is getting cheaper. However, new technology is also making it possible to extend medical treatment into new areas, and thus increase health costs.

Throughout industrial development, new technology increased productivity and reduced labour costs. As new industries have emerged, so have new skills (Frey, 2019; 2020). There is no logical reason why a similar development will not occur in the Fourth Industrial Revolution, and in the healthcare sector that we are examining here. If this assumption is correct, then we will see increasing productivity and skills development in the healthcare sector. It is precisely this increase in productivity in the healthcare sector that will to some extent alleviate some of the problems related to increased costs. We are not saying that costs will be reduced overall, because the ageing population and new medical treatments will push costs up. However, there will be a relative reduction in costs in relation to the increased utilization of AI and robotics.

Historically, increased productivity has also resulted in increased wages. This can partly explain why both employee and employer organizations have agreed to promote the technological development of work processes, even though this can lead to increased automation, loss of jobs, and the need for retraining. In the healthcare sector, this development may also occur in the future. Productivity growth will result in wage increases. However, increased productivity will not necessarily result in a reduction in labour because of the lack of "first line competence." In other words, productivity increase as a result of new technology will enable more healthcare workers to stay in the profession, and those workers who have left the healthcare industry may return due to increased wage levels and improved working conditions. In this way, AI and robotics will increase productivity and wage levels in the healthcare sector. This development will most likely result in more "first line competence" being available to those who need it, which will emphasize the fact that "humans are underrated."

Based on the above narrative, description, analysis, theoretical reflections and the review of practical utility, we have developed a Boudon–Coleman diagram,

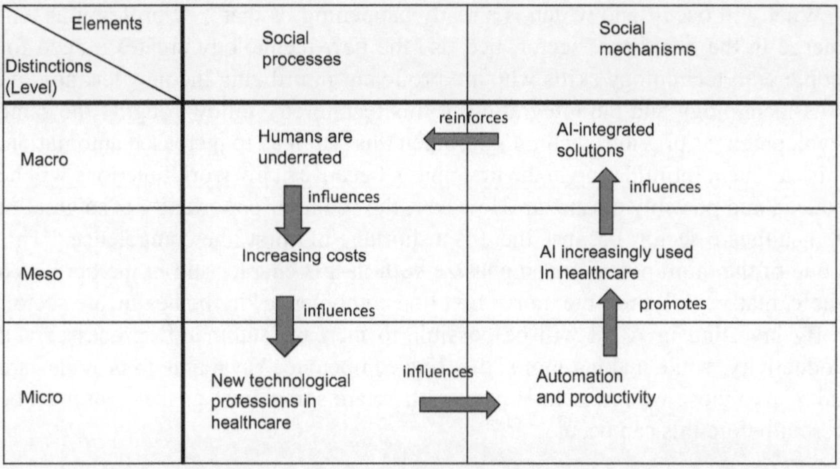

Figure 3.3 AI and opportunities in the healthcare sector: A Boudon–Coleman diagram.

which illustrates some of the relationships we have discussed in this chapter (Figure 3.3).

Conclusion

In this chapter, we have examined the following question: What are the opportunities for using AI in the healthcare sector?

We have discussed how mobile health can improve quality in the healthcare sector and increase the productivity of healthcare workers. Mobile health, especially when coupled to artificial intelligence, is an important social mechanism for promoting the focus on the healthcare professions, and at the same time improving the quality of the services provided. In this chapter, we have also emphasized that although high technology in general, and artificial intelligence in particular, are being increasingly used, it is "first line competence" that will be of decisive importance for maintaining the quality of healthcare services.

We have also emphasized the importance of integrated AI solutions. It is only when we are able to integrate this technology that quality can be increased and the performance of healthcare workers improved. When integrated AI solutions are implemented, this will affect costs. In the first phase, costs will increase, because people will work side by side with the new technology. However, over time, employees will gain new AI skills enabling increased productivity.

What we have seen with all technology in the past is that as the learning curve increases, costs decrease because productivity increases. However, it is important to stress that productivity will most likely fall first, costs will increase, and resistance to these changes will also increase. It is only when a certain skill level is achieved in the application of the new technology that productivity increases, costs fall and resistance to changes diminishes in strength.

What will occur, and which is already happening, is that new professions will emerge in the healthcare sector, because the new technology creates a need for people with technology skills who are proficient in utilizing the new technology. If AI technology and the integration of this technology follow roughly the same development as previous technologies, then this will lead to increased automation. This can seem intimidating in the first phase, because many work functions will be reduced and possibly disappear. However, the scope of opportunity is so great in the healthcare sector, because there is a shortage of "first line competence." This is one of the main points we emphasize both in this chapter and in the book as a whole, that AI will promote more "first line competence" in the healthcare sector.

By investing in AI, it will be possible to increase automation processes and productivity, while making more "first line competence" available to provide care and help to those who need it. However, there are some prerequisites that must be present before this can occur.

1. One important prerequisite is that there is political will to improve the health system.
2. Another important prerequisite is that a policy is developed which is aimed at encouraging health professionals who have left the healthcare sector to return to the sector. Such a policy can focus on creating various types of incentives, such as improved working hours, working conditions, and pay.
3. A third prerequisite is the importance of establishing training programmes related to the integration and application of the new technology.
4. A fourth prerequisite is that both the political system and the administrative system need to be aware of the fact that costs will first increase, and then decrease over time. It is this time gap between costs increasing, and until they decrease, because productivity increases, that decision-makers need to come to terms with when implementing policies.
5. The fifth prerequisite is that those people who work at the overall policy level need to be aware of the fact that there is not a causal relationship between new technology and productivity growth. This relationship, on the other hand, is dependent on political, administrative, and management decision-making; i.e., it is necessary to optimize organization, in order to increase productivity. If this does not occur, it is highly probable that costs will continue to rise, even when the integration of AI increases in strength.
6. A crucial prerequisite is the need to understand that if we manage to increase productivity in both the healthcare sector, and in the economy as a whole, with the help of AI-integrated solutions, then we will have more resources available to address various social needs, both in the healthcare sector, and in other sectors of the economy.
7. If innovation processes come to a halt, and productivity declines, then we will face major challenges. Therefore, it is an important prerequisite for promoting the opportunities of using AI in the healthcare sector that we stimulate innovation processes at all levels in society.

Notes

1 Carou et al., 2022; Esposito, 2022; Flynn, 2019; Lidstrømer, & Ashrafian, 2022; Li, 2020; Mahajan, 2021; Motylsky et al., 2021; Reddy, 2021; Saxena et al., 2021; Topol, 2019; Xing et al., 2020.
2 https://www.intechopen.com/chapters/60562
3 https://link.springer.com/chapter/10.1007/978-3-319-94878-2_4
4 https://en.wikipedia.org/wiki/Alan_Turing
5 https://en.wikipedia.org/wiki/Warren_Sturgis_McCulloch
https://en.wikipedia.org/wiki/Walter_Pitts
6 https://en.wikipedia.org/wiki/Frank_Rosenblatt
7 https://en.wikipedia.org/wiki/Connectionism
8 https://en.wikipedia.org/wiki/Cybernetics
9 https://en.wikipedia.org/wiki/Deep_learning
10 https://en.wikipedia.org/wiki/ChatGPT
11 https://www.theaaih.org/news/blog-post-title-one-xrepm-9xbyd-sy8eb
12 https://www.intechopen.com/chapters/60562
13 https://journals.plos.org/plosone/article?id=10.1371/journal.pone.0151470
14 https://www.thelancet.com/journals/landig/article/PIIS2589-7500(19)30063-9/fulltext
15 https://ieeexplore.ieee.org/abstract/document/8877113?casa_token=gMWZxRPN96kAAAAA:ghllLi63wE9YePKPcPOct7R4BMA7aexC6z1jhRqYH8hHhmDv8wZc9Ux4TgnkhiqwHU_srXrDMH2qoZg
16 https://books.google.dk/books?hl=en&lr=&id=_EFlDwAAQBAJ&oi=fnd&pg=PT7&dq=ai+where+is+the+human+in+healthcare&ots=BI8yt__A8U&sig=tb8Krd9-Laf5qMpcN35Z8tc3VOM&redir_esc=y#v=onepage&q=ai%20where%20is%20the%20human%20in%20healthcare&f=false
17 Frey, 2019; 2020; Broedberry & Fukao, 2021; Cippola, 1971; Carr, 2022; North, 1981; Roncaglia, 2019; Scheidel, 2018; Schumpeter, 1954; Shah et al., 2014.
18 https://www.sciencedirect.com/science/article/pii/S156816371830240X
19 https://journals.sagepub.com/doi/pdf/10.1177/15553434221129914?casa_token=pJ0WvDjUxnYAAAAA:YE3GdfYQ3A1wTnNhadafv6jKcA8hmnHmrlWl0AOq01CcQi6oOx1PQlLxw3wEyQILW2LlaBrJODzxoXw
20 https://journals.sagepub.com/doi/pdf/10.1177/15553434221129914?casa_token=pJ0WvDjUxnYAAAAA:YE3GdfYQ3A1wTnNhadafv6jKcA8hmnHmrlWl0AOq01CcQi6oOx1PQlLxw3wEyQILW2LlaBrJODzxoXw
21 https://journals.sagepub.com/doi/pdf/10.1177/15553434221129914?casa_token=AW5wBq7R0RkAAAAA:DhnAZoa7iKnY0Atc7GitUytlHYzOQ4DfG7u3DDE8TTtRN4ptJ7TfIt_lSE9xu6ZpHQi-R6dY404APms
22 https://www.tandfonline.com/doi/full/10.1080/07317115.2022.2043977
23 https://en.wikipedia.org/wiki/MHealth
24 "Intelligent informats" refer to intelligent robots that are networked to all relevant expertise within a specific field, e.g., within healthcare services.

References

Allaban, A.A.; Wang, M. & Padır, T. (2020). A systematic review of robotics research in support of in-home care for older adults, *Information*, 11(2), 75. https://doi.org/10.3390/info11020075

Al-Turmjan, F.; Kumar, M.; Staphany, T. & Bhardwaj, A. (2022). *Evolving role of AI and IoMT in the health care market*, Springer, London.

Ashby, W.R. (1961). *An introduction to cybernetics*, Chapman & Hall LTD, New York.

Ashby, W.R. (1970). Connectance of large dynamic (cybernetic) systems: Critical values for stability, *Nature*, 228(5273, 21 November).

Ashby, W.R. (1981). What is an intelligent machine? in Conant, R. (ed.), *Mechanisms of Intelligence*, Intersystems Seaside.
Asplund, J. (1970). *Om undran innfør samhället*, Argos, Stockholm.
Asplund, J. (2010). *Det sociala livets elementära former*, Korpen, Stockholm.
Baumol, W.J. (2012). *The cost disease: Why computers get cheaper and health care doesn't*, Yale University Press, New Haven.
Billington, D.P. (2020). *From insight to innovation*, MIT Press, Boston.
Bohr, A. & Memarzadeh, K. (2020). *Artificial intelligence in healthcare*, Academic Press, New York.
Boyraz, P.; Dobrev, I.; Fisher, G. & Popovic, M.B. (2019). Robot surgery, in Popovic, M.B. (ed.), *Biomechatronics*, Academic Press, London, pp. 431–450.
Britnell, M. (2019). *Human: Solving the global workforce crises in healthcare*, Oxford University Press, Oxford.
Broedberry, S. & Fukao, K. (2021). *The Cambridge economic history of the modern world*, Cambridge University Press, Cambridge.
Carey, N. (2019). *Hacking the code of life: How gene editing will rewrite our futures*, Icon Books, New York.
Carou, D.; Sartal, A. & Darim, J.P. (2022). *Machine learning and artificial intelligence with industrial applications: From big data to small data*, Springer, London.
Carr, C.H. (2022). *What is history?* Penguin, New York.
Cippola, C.M. (1971). *The Fontana economic history of Europe*, Fontana Books, London.
Drucker, P.F. (1999). Knowledge worker productivity: The biggest challenge, *California Management Review*, 41(2), 79–94.
Drucker, P.F. (1999a). *Management challenges for the 21st century*, Harper Collins, New York.
Esposito, E. (2022). *Artificial communication: How algorithms produce social intelligence*, The MIT Press, Boston.
Flynn, A. (2019). Using artificial intelligence in health-system pharmacy practice: Finding new patterns that matter, *American Journal of Health System Pharmacy*, 76(9), 622–627.
Frey, C.B. (2019). *The technology trap: Capital, labor, and power in the age of automation*, Princeton University Press, Princeton.
Frey, C.B. (2020). Attitudes towards technology: Part II, in Skidelsky, R. & Craig, N. (eds.), *Work in the future: The automation revolution*, Palgrave, London, pp. 89–97.
Hamel, G. (2007). *The future of management*, Harvard Business School Press, Boston.
Hamel, G. (2008). Introduction, in Skarzynski, P. & Gibson, R. (eds.), *Innovation to the core*, Harvard Business Press, Boston, pp. xvii–xix.
Hamel, G. (2012). *What matters now: How to win in a world of relentless change ferocious competition, and unstoppable innovation*, John Wiley & Sons, New York.
Househ, M.; Borycki, E. & Kushniruk, A. (2021). *Multiple perspectives on artificial intelligence in healthcare, opportunities and challenges*, Springer.
Johannessen, J-A. (2021). *China's innovation economy: Artificial Intelligence and the new silk road*, Routledge, London.
Johannessen, J-A. (2022). *The New Silk Road and the innovation economy in china*, Routledge, London.
Kurzweil, R. (2005). *The singularity is near*, Penguin, London.
Kurzweil, R. (2008). *The age of spiritual machines: When computers exceed human intelligence*, Penguin, London.
Kurzweil, R. (2013). *How to create a mind: The secret of human thought revealed*, Penguin Books, New York.
Li, R. (2020). *Artificial intelligence revolution: How AI will change our society, economy and culture*, Skyhorse Publishing, New York.
Lidstrømer, N. & Ashrafian, A. (2022). *Artificial intelligence in medicine*, Springer, London.
Mahajan, P.S. (2021). *Artificial intelligence in healthcare*, MedMantra, New Mexico.

Motulsky, A.; Nikiema, J-N. & Bosson-Rieutort, D. (2021). Artificial intelligence and medication management, in Househ, M.; Borycki, E. & Kushniruk, A. (eds.), *Multiple perspectives on artificial intelligence in healthcare*, Springer, pp. 91–101.

North, D.C. (1981). *Structure and change in economic history*, Norton, New York.

Porter, M.E. & Teisberg, E.O. (2006). *Redefining health care: Creating value-based competition on results*, Harvard Business School Press, Boston.

Pu, L.; Moyle, W.; Jones, C. & Todorovic, M. (2019). The effectiveness of social robots for older adults: A systematic review and meta- analysis of randomized controlled studies. *The Gerontologist*, 59(1), Article e37–e51. https://doi.org/10.1093/geront/gny046

Reddy, S. (2021). Algorithmic medicine, in Reddy, S. (ed.), *Artificial Intelligence: Application in healthcare delivery*, Routledge, London, pp. 1–14.

Roncaglia, A. (2019). *The age of fragmentation: A history of contemporary economic thought*, Cambridge University Press, Cambridge.

Russel, S. & Norvig, P. (2016). *Artificial intelligence: A modern approach*, Pearson, New York.

Sanchez-Vives, M.V. & Slater, M. (2005). From presence to consciousness through virtual reality, *Nature Reviews Neuroscience*, 6(4), 332–339.

Saxena, A.; Saxena, M.; Deo, A. & Llerena, A.R. (2021). Transformation of mHealth in society, in Saxena, A.; Brault, N. & Rashid, S. (eds.), *Big data and artificial intelligence for healthcare applications*, CRC Press, London, pp. 165–193.

Scheidel, W. (2018). *The great leveler: Violence and the history of inequality from the stone age to the twenty-first century*, Princeton University Press, Princeton.

Schumpeter, J. (1954). *History of economic analysis*, Oxford University Press, Oxford.

Shah, J.; Vyas, A. & Vyas, D. (2014). The history of robotics in surgical specialities, *American Journal of Robotic Surgery*, 1(1), 12–20.

Shridhar, A.N.; Briggs, T.P.; Kelly, J.D. & Nathan, S. (2017). Training in robotic surgery: An overview, *Current Urology Reports*, 18, 58. https://doi.org/10.1007/s11934-017-0710-y

Sidey-Gibbons, J.A.M. & Sidey-Gibbons, C.J. (2019). Machine learning in medicine: A practical introduction, *BMC Medical Research Methodology*, 19(1), 1–18.

Simon, H.A. (1965). *The shape of automation for men and management*, Harper & Row, New York.

Simon, H.A. (2019). *The science of the artificial: Reissue of the third edition with a new introduction by John Laird*, MIT Press, Boston.

Sqalli, M.T.; Al-Thani, D.; Qaraqw, M. & Fernandez-Kuque, L. (2021). Perspectives on Human-AI interaction applied to health and wellness management: Between milestones and hurdles, in Househ, M.; Borycki, E. & Kushniruk, A. (eds.), *Multiple perspectives on artificial intelligence in healthcare, opportunities and challenges*, Springer, pp. 41–51.

Topol, E.J. (2019). High-performance medicine: The convergence of human and artificial intelligence, *Nature Medicine*, 25(1), 44–56.

Villaronga, E.F. & Drukarch, H. (2022). *AI for Healthcare robotics*, CRC Press, London.

Wachter, R. (2015). *The digital doctor*, McGraw Hill, New York.

Wong, P.S.S. (2013). *Drucker's knowledge-worker productivity theory*, Lambert Academic Publishing, Saarbrucken.

Woods, T. (2020). *Live longer with AI*, Packt, Birmingham.

Xing, L.; Giger, M.L. & Min, J.K. (2020). *Artificial intelligence in medicine: Technical basis and clinical applications*, Academic Press, New York.

4 A systemic perspective on the philosophy of medicine

Core idea

Philosophy is an essential component of the medical profession.

Key points

- As scientific trials became more common, objectivity became an essential component of medical treatment.
- In order to prescribe the appropriate medical interventions, it is necessary to identify the causal mechanisms.
- Medical ethics have a direct impact on medical practice.
- Historically, medical norms have been slow to change. As a result, doctors may continue to prescribe outdated treatments.
- Pharmaceutical companies may prioritize efforts to develop drugs and treatments according to their potential for generating profit, rather than the extent of human need.
- What we know is conditioned by how we came to know it.
- Tacit knowledge, e.g., a nurse's clinical gaze, is subjective in its existence, but objective in its consequences.

Introduction

Most medical professionals apply philosophical assumptions in their practice, even if they are not aware of doing so. For example, many will assume that health challenges are caused by specific physical conditions, rather than social constructs. While this may often be true, this is not the point we are making here. Our point is that medical professionals' reasoning is based on philosophical assumptions. Most medical professionals take a rational approach and look for the causes of disease. Such an approach is philosophical, as the logical causal assumption is precisely a philosophical understanding of the ontology or assumed reality that surrounds us. When these professionals assume that their practice and experience have provided them with knowledge, which they can then apply to their patients, they are making an epistemological assumption (epistemology being one of the core areas of philosophy).

DOI: 10.4324/9781003497325-5

When doctors, nurses, and other professionals in the healthcare sector assume that the hypotheses they have need to be checked against the facts, they base this on a methodological foundation, which is an important part of philosophy. When the same professionals consider whether a patient should be given treatment that will burden the hospital budget and possibly negatively affect other patients, then the health professionals are involved in ethical assessments. Ethics is also an essential part of philosophy. When these professionals consider the right values to relate to, they are using another branch of philosophy, at least in relation to a systemic understanding of philosophy, namely axiology. Against this background, it can be said that healthcare personnel, whatever their understanding and interest in philosophy, use philosophical reasoning in their medical practice. According to systemic thinking, philosophy is divided into the following areas: Ontology, epistemology, methodology, ethics, and axiology.

One can probably claim that philosophical discussions are not the type of discussions that are most explicitly prevalent in the healthcare sector. On the other hand, we have tried to point out that on a more fundamental and unspoken level, medical practice is closely related to general philosophical questions. Making explicit what is used in practice, but which is not so clearly stated, can be advantageous in relation to future health challenges, health workers, and not least the patients.

We know that many concepts are socially constructed. For example, the concepts of "living on a bare minimum" or being poor. These socially constructed concepts will differ in meaning from country to country, and for different groups and people. In contrast, malnutrition and hunger are not socially constructed. They exist as phenomena in the real world, and can have consequences for people's health. Both malnutrition and hunger can be measured by blood tests and other objective methods; although hunger can also be a subjective experience, it is real and objective in its consequences. We also know that the technology that becomes part of the healthcare system affects social systems, such as hospitals and other systems in which it is used. Technology affects social systems at various levels, such as the individual, group, organizational, and societal levels. This is why healthcare systems must also take this socio-technological phenomenon into account when considering the implementation of artificial intelligence. Furthermore, this socio-technological aspect is related to the empirical data and the social laws that are adopted as a result of the application of technology. The empirical data used in our health systems affect, and is also affected by, the medical trials that more or less continuously take place in health systems. However, these medical trials are limited by the medical ethics and medical axiology we have referred to above.

Empirical data and medical trials are important so that the medical profession does not succumb to the temptation of using what Hippocrates called "postulates," i.e., assumptions that have not been tested by using scientific method (Bunge, 2013: viii). We see here that how knowledge is developed, i.e., the epistemological system in philosophy, has an impact on how healthcare workers relate to their profession. This knowledge is as important today as it was in Hippocrates' time.

Our point with this introduction has been to show that, whether one is interested in it or not, philosophy is an essential part of the medical profession.

Narratives

Case letter 1: Are healthcare systems conservative in their use of technology?

Digitalization is advancing extremely rapidly in the healthcare sector. The sector's complexity is causing many setbacks in the digitalization process, however. Despite these problems, digitalization will become a dominant feature of future healthcare systems as more sophisticated mobile networks, e.g., 5G (and 6G in the future), become available. It is paradoxical that the sector that should benefit most from the adoption of digital technologies is inherently sluggish in applying them. In 2019, e.g., the British government had to order the National Health Service (NHS) to stop buying fax machines and end their use by 2020.[1] Although the use of fax machines was outdated, the rate of change in the NHS was so slow that government action was needed to hasten the adoption of new technology that was already widespread in other sectors in the United Kingdom. We highlight this example in this case letter, because a medical philosophy based on systemic thinking requires the application of cutting-edge technology, in order to promote the optimal development of healthcare systems.

Digital healthcare, telemedicine, and AI will most likely be crucial for tackling the many challenges that exist in the healthcare sector. The use in the NHS of antiquated fax machines underlines how one's mindset towards technology has consequences for the development of future healthcare systems. We can see that ideologies have a direct impact on strategies for developing future healthcare systems. We would also assert that fields that have historically been slow to change are holding healthcare systems back from utilizing the latest technology.

The tendency to use archaic solutions within the health systems is changing around the world. A large survey shows that in the United States and some European countries, such as The Netherlands, digital healthcare is developing relatively quickly.[2] The same survey reports that AI and digital solutions within the health industry are increasing, e.g., for diagnoses, wearable health monitoring devices, virtual appointments, and so on. It is probable that artificial intelligence, in its various applications, will become an integral part of the future technology in health systems around the world, although there are many commentators who are critical of such a development.

Although there is much evidence that artificial intelligence will become an integral part of future health systems, the example of the archaic fax machines is something one should be aware of, because it signals a conservative attitude towards new technology in the health sector, at least in the United Kingdom. It seems that there has not been enough investment in basic technological architectures, around which the new technology will be built. Thus many systems are weighed down by outdated applications that do not interact well with other applications, so that operations are slow and siloed. It is in this context that a medical systemic philosophy can be useful, because context competence and part-whole understanding are some of the foundations of a medical systemic philosophy (Bunge, 2013).

In the situation described in this case letter, it is possible that an increasing competition between various healthcare agencies and institutions is not the right medicine, because the new technology requires cooperation rather than competition. While competition can be appropriate when you want to keep down costs, it is conceivable that cooperation will be a better approach when the purpose is to fully integrate various technologies with each other. Competitive tendering makes sense when the health service wishes to cut costs, but in social systems that are built on cooperation, it is not always the best strategy. Collaborative solutions are needed when the aim is to promote technological integration and information sharing across different technological platforms and across different professions and levels in the healthcare sector.

Case letter 2: The philosophy of social science – systemic thinking and the positivist position

Understanding, explanation, and predication (wherever possible) will, as far as systemic thinking is concerned, always be oriented towards deeper contexts and therefore the construction of new patterns. It is the pattern which combines (Bateson, 1972) that systemic thinkers are always looking for when dealing with scientific problems/phenomena. It is the construction and synthesis that constitute the search object for systemic thinking. Analysis is purely a tool, in order to achieve this. If the analysis is given precedence, the construction and synthesis will lag behind. In systemic thinking, science is a moral project (Bunge, 1989). If science is not constructed as a moral project, it will not only lose its legitimacy, but also its direction, which is the search for truth, and can thus be a means for achieving unethical goals.

Systemic thinking and the positivist position

In the following, we will discuss empiricism and positivism. While Hempel and Carnap can be perceived as positivists, Popper can be perceived as a rationalist (Bunge, 1996). Positivists have in common a disregard for subjective experience, particularly emotions and intentions, as well as political and economic perspectives.

EMPIRICISM

Empiricists have a bias in relation to constructs that are not in full accordance with the data they represent. It is only a perception, i.e., what can be observed in the literal sense of the word, which provides knowledge for empiricists. "Naive empiricists" collect and process data in the computer era in enormous quantities, without being able to generate any theories, which one might expect regarding the enormous efforts invested (see Turner, 1991).

Empiricists hold the view that knowledge comes primarily from sensory experience. The objection to this view is that in order to gain knowledge from experience reflection is necessary; however, the reflection process presupposes the design of constructs (concepts, models, theories), which are not necessarily a product of experience, such as "truth," consistency, conceptual models, relations, information, social systems, justice, and so on. In other words, concepts cannot be "experienced," and a theory can definitely not be "experienced." Theories are constructed by researchers, and then various hypotheses can be tested in relation to the theory. These are non-empirical concepts, a fact that has been acknowledged by the neo-positivists.

There are two main types of empiricists: Positivists and neo-positivists (logical empiricists).

Positivism and neo-positivism

The origin of logical empiricism (or neo-positivism) is associated with the Vienna Circle (1926–1936). The main focus was on empirical testability and induction, in addition to perceptual data, as the basis for knowledge development. Logical empiricism refers to a philosophical movement that is characterized by the view that scientific knowledge is the only kind of factual knowledge.[3] The main idea was the unity of science. However, logical empiricism dwindled in popularity after Kuhn's *The Structure of the Scientific Revolutions* (Kuhn, 1976). Since then, positivism and logical empiricism have often been viewed as being of purely academic interest. On the other hand, this philosophical movement has been covertly held in high esteem by many scientists, or in Bunge's words (1996: 317) it is "the tacit philosophy of many scientists."

Positivists are empiricists in the sense that they stay very close to observable data, so close that they do not make the distinction between the epistemological and the ontological. This brings about a distrust in theories; consequently, positivists do not have synthesis as their goal for scientific development.

Positivists do not make a distinction between the epistemological and the ontological, but take the ontological for granted. Therefore the maxim for them will be rhetorically expressed: To count, weigh, measure, and then to know. The ethical dimension for the positivists will then be irrelevant in relation to science, since ethics cannot be quantified. Positivists will, in the wider sense, ignore axiology and ethics in their scientific projects (Bunge, 1996, 1998, 2001).

In cultural science it was Comte who initiated the positivist debate. Comte's "ultimate ambition was to be a champion of the positive scientific spirit in the study of social phenomenon" (Von Wright, 1971: 171). Comte's basis, in his use of scientific methods in physics, is known by the name he originally gave to what became sociology, namely "social physics" (Urmson & Ree, 1989: 63). Comte's doctrines for positivism were, according to Habermas (1968: 77):

1 Empirical science is only one form of knowledge, but the only source of positive knowledge.
2 Emphasizing technical control of society.

According to Von Wright (1971: 4), the positivists in the natural sciences and social sciences have the following in common:

- Methodological unity.
- Mathematical/statistical orientation.

- Linear causal explanations.
- Hypothetical deductive statements based on universal laws and/or statistical laws.

Explanations of a non-linear causal type, such as intention, purpose, expectation and motive, were, and are still, viewed by the positivists, as being unscientific, and not considered in scientific contexts (Von Wright, 1971: 4).

In this context, there is a clear-cut distinction between systemic thinking and the positivist school. In systemic thinking, the distinction is made between intention and behaviour, where intention can be explained in relation to social consequences. Circular causal processes are also emphasized as well as linear causal processes.

Regardless of the types of problems treated in the social sciences (hard and soft), criticism from the systemic position against the positivist position emphasizes that the latter only to a limited extent problematizes the distinction between the described and the description, i.e., the epistemological and ontological distinction. Another criticism is concerned with the way science is turned into a question of procedural rules and discussions about methods. We further criticize the positivist position for omitting moral/ethical considerations in terms of results and consequences in relation to science. It is, however, the absence of an epistemological debate which appears to be characteristic of the positivist position in the social sciences.

Description related to medical philosophy

In this description, we will elaborate on five elements. These five elements, which are systemically related as shown in Figure 4.1, are the following: Health as a social construction, sociotechnology (the link between the health systems and technology), empirical data and social laws, scientific medical trials and finally, medical ethics.

HEALTH AS A SOCIAL CONSTRUCTION

One can of course take the perspective that medicine is not related to philosophy. However, as we have shown in Case Letter 2, we have seen that when you start with "facts" and empirical evidence, you have already taken a philosophical perspective. Whether one is aware of this or not is a completely different matter. When we say here that health is a social construct, this needs a little elaboration. It is of course not social facts that are constructed, but symbols, narratives, and metaphors that are socially constructed. These dimensions then in turn affect the social system. It is precisely the distinction between the epistemological and the ontological that is essential for understanding how symbols, metaphors, and narratives affect the ontological area, something we tried to show in Case Letter 2. However, the text does not replace social facts, such as Derrida seems to think (Baird, 2023). The text affects and is affected by social facts, and that is something quite different.

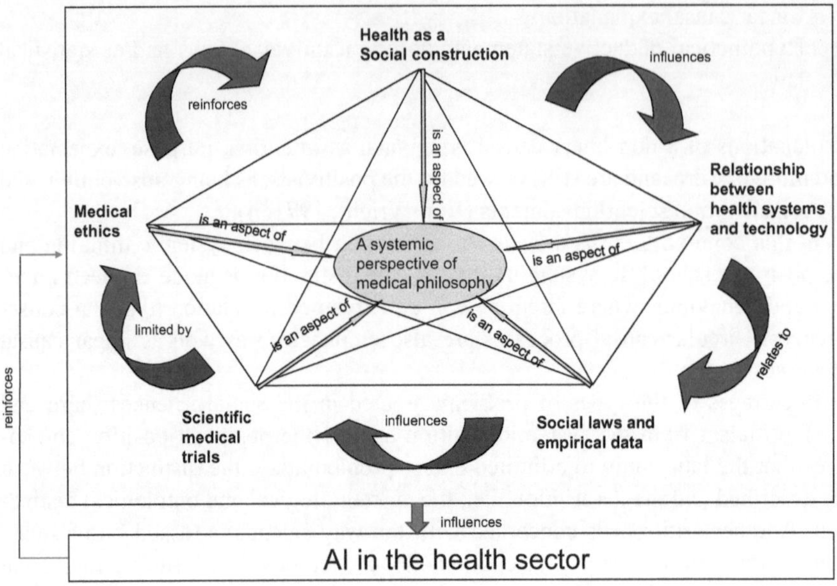

Figure 4.1 Medical philosophy: A systemic perspective.

It is the confusion between reality and the representation of reality which, in systemic thinking, constitutes the objection to ontological constructivism, not the obvious fact that constructs are constructed. Facts are not constructed. On the other hand, constructs about social facts are constructions, but this is something entirely different. The truth is neither a fact, a datum, nor a construction. Truth in a scientific context is the relation between facts and the construct/constructs, and there are several constructs that can be true about the same fact, hence the systemic denotation "partial truth."

Any fact (facts), e.g., Knut drinks alcohol every day includes:

A A specific thing: Alcohol.
B A property of the thing; i.e., the consumption of alcohol leads to intoxication upon the ingestion of a certain quantity.
C A change in state; i.e., from sober to a degree of intoxication.
D A pattern; i.e., ingestion of alcohol every day.
E A social law; i.e., consumption of alcohol every day leads to (in all probability) alcoholism, which excludes Knut from much of social life, e.g., working life.

Social facts can be organized into economic, political, cultural, and biological entities and relations between these entities. The constructs about these entities are indefinite.

Any property: Property pertaining to the thing, relation property, core property, accidental property, original property, and deduced property of certain constructs, are, per definition, constructed (by the human mind). Systems of properties are in the same way as constructs meant to say something about social reality. Construct logic (or predicate logic) must therefore not be confused with causal relations in social reality. They are two domains distinctly different, operating according to their own mechanisms.

According to the systemic position, it is a misconception to say that facts are social constructs. The misunderstanding implies that we confuse our concepts about facts and our hypotheses about facts together with facts. Our concepts and hypotheses are mental constructs. Facts, on the other hand, are not mental constructs.

POVERTY IS A SOCIAL FACT, WHILE MALNUTRITION IS A 'FACT'

For the fishermen, it is a fact that either they were able to catch fish or unable to catch fish. The fisherman's "feeling of freedom" in his fishing boat at sea is predominately a mental construct.

For the farmer, it is a fact that either it rains on his land, or it does not rain on his land. Whether or not the farmer perceives himself as an independent businessman, like other owners of small businesses, is a social construction. All mental and social constructions can be changed by those using them.

Not being able to read is a social fact. Illiteracy on the other hand is a social construction. Hypotheses are meant to function as a link between social constructions and facts. A confusion of mental and social constructions, and what these are meant to represent, will result in confusion in the social sciences.

A symbol can symbolize something, in the same way that a concept can describe something. A hypothesis is aimed at explaining something, or expressing something about contexts. A conceptual model is aimed at expressing something about relations between concepts, and a theory is about the relations of propositions. Physical or social facts are not affected by mental constructions.

THE LINK BETWEEN THE HEALTH SYSTEMS AND TECHNOLOGY

Modern medicine is characterized by scientific research. Medical research also involves philosophical challenges. As we have shown above, one of these challenges will be based on whether we have confidence in our observations. Is what we observe a social construction or something that is true based on certain scientific criteria? Most people assume that what they observe is true. However, this assumption is based on modern logic, which excludes myths. On the basis of this reflection, we can say that technology becomes part of the medical philosophy of health systems. How can we know that the technological solutions offered are the best for the patients, the elderly, the disabled, or if this technology has only been developed because it gives the biggest profit to those who sell this technology? Evidence-based medicine (launched in 1991) represents a new way of thinking, which can be related to many of the questions raised in the previous part. Evidence-based medicine (EBM) can be largely contrasted with only focusing on an individual's observations and personal experiences. Evidence-based medicine is based on using the current best evidence and scientific information in clinical management. It is in this context that sociotechnology becomes an important addition to medical philosophy from a systemic perspective.

The term "sociotechnology" has been attributed to Mario Bunge (1998: 297–455). Sociotechnology is the study of processes at the intersection of society and technology. For health systems, this concerns the technological solutions that are used in health systems, and how technology and health systems have mutually influenced each other's development. Sociotechnology in health systems may be defined as all the activities and processes that use technology to perform health tasks. Understood in this way, it is important to study sociotechnology, in order to promote the goals we have for health systems; in other words, both the technological and social processes need to be investigated. More specifically, this applies to hospitals, aged care, people with disabilities, and so on. Sociotechnology applied to health systems is thus an integral part of medical philosophy considered from a systemic perspective.

The aim of sociotechnology in general is to design social systems where the technology is decisive for a system's effectiveness, as well as to develop methods for evaluation and corrections to the implemented technology and its management. Specifically, Bunge (2013: 297) says that the study of sociotechnology is:

> the ways of maintaining, repairing, improving, or replacing existing social systems (e.g. factories, hospitals, schools) and processes (e.g. manufacture, healthcare, and education); (…) and it designs and redesigns social systems and processes to tackle social issues (e.g. mass unemployment, epidemics and crime).

He says further that sociotechnology is on a par with electrical engineering, biotechnology, and knowledge engineering.

The aim of sociotechnology for health systems is more specifically to design, evaluate, and correct the effect of measures introduced at different levels. The interaction and investigation of social processes and technology in, e.g., hospitals can help us understand, explain, and possibly solve some of the health challenges of the future. Specifically, this investigation can, in relation to the new emerging technology, such as artificial intelligence, help us to understand some of the positive and negative consequences of using this technology.

SOCIAL LAWS AND EMPIRICAL DATA

Social laws constitute a pattern of a unique type. They are systemic and connected to a system of knowledge and cannot change without the facts they represent also being changed (Bunge, 1983; 1983a). The main differences between a statement of a law and other statements are:

1 Law statements are general.
2 Law statements are systemic, i.e., they are related to the established system of knowledge.
3 Law statements have been verified through many studies.

A pattern may be understood as variables that are stable over a specific period of time. A social law is created when an observer gains insight into the pattern. By gaining such insight, we can also predict parts of behaviour, or at least develop a rough estimate within a short period of time.

Social laws are further related to specific social systems, both in time and space. However, this does not represent any objection to social laws, because this is also true of natural laws (although these have a longer time span and are of a more general nature).

Social laws are based on empirical data. It is this empirical data that are used when medical research strives to create evidence-based knowledge. The emphasis on rigour using empirical data is a counterweight to the individual's clinical experiences and observations, or what goes by the name of "clinical gaze." However, we should add that the "clinical gaze" can be decisive in cases where empirical data are insufficient or does not exist, and where tacit knowledge is prominent (Polanyi, 1966; 1969; 2015).

Evidence-based methods are nothing new in medical methodology. They have been used since the time of Hippocrates. The point, however, is that methods have been constantly improved, and will probably continue to be improved in the future. Another point is that these methods stand in contrast to phenomenological and hermeneutic methods. It is therefore not the lack of focus on empirical data that can explain why medical research has not progressed. It is the belief in shamans, myths, subjective methodology, and irrational methods that have been a problem and a challenge for medical research.

Empirical data collected and analyzed by various evidence-based methods will ensure a development of medical practice. Evidence-based research in medicine is 2,000 years old, and originates from Hippocrates' first empirical experiments (Bunge, 2013: 28). It is possible that it is not only shamans and myths that are a challenge to medical philosophy and the clinical improvements of practice. It is conceivable that medical economics is also a similar challenge. The rationale is that there is a goal conflict between evidence-based research in health research on the one hand, and the economic methods that have come to be used in decision-making processes in health systems, on the other hand. We will not reflect more on this conflict of goals, but simply note that this may represent a potential destructive force in health systems.

In a philosophical reflection, it may be important to reflect on the concept of evidence-based research. In this context, we say that empirical data are the basis for this research. However, this is not a correct statement, because empirical data are inherently neutral; they say nothing until they are confronted with an assumption. An assumption in a scientific context is a hypothesis. It is when a hypothesis is confronted with empirical data that we can develop new knowledge, or disprove old knowledge. For example, the fact that the average weight of men has increased in recent years can be seen as an empirical datum. It doesn't tell us much more than just this. It is only when we develop the hypothesis that such a development will lead to increased diabetes in the population in the future that we have developed the basis for new knowledge. The knowledge is of course not materialized by the development of the hypothesis, but by testing the hypothesis. The point of this brief reflection is that empirical data are only medically interesting after they are confronted with a hypothesis, which is then tested against empirical data.

SCIENTIFIC MEDICAL TRIALS

Clinical therapies are created on the basis of various scientific trials, as well as empirical data obtained from these trials. In this way, medical trials become part of a process for developing clinical therapies. Medical trials are based on recognized and established scientific methods, in order to ensure objectivity in the results. It is this objectivity that ensures that various types of shamans, healers, and so on, no longer have such a dominant place in medicine. With the breakthrough of scientific thinking, subjective experiences were also downplayed. However, it can also be said that subjective experiences are based on a type of empirical data regarding treatment, but only to a certain extent. After all, subjective experiences were an improvement in relation to the type of treatments used by a shaman, or in religious rituals. As scientific trials became more common, objectivity became an essential component of medical treatment. Although scientific trials represented an advance in medical development, scientific methods are also under constant development. All scientific research is based on existing knowledge. However, this knowledge is constantly evolving. Therefore, the medical forms of treatment will also be under constant development. As new knowledge changes established knowledge, medical treatments will also change in character. The credibility of any medical treatment is based on the quality and scientific level of the medical trials on which the treatment is based. These assumptions exist long before the medical trials start. Therefore, the knowledge that exists in a medical environment is crucial for whether the clinical trials are designed at the best available level of knowledge in relation to methodology and professional medical competence.

It is important in this context to establish that experience is different from data obtained from scientific experiments. Experiences are subjective, even if intersubjectivity should exist between several people who have similar experiences. Scientific experiments are subject to completely different scientific control mechanisms, and the results are therefore objective. They are objective in the sense that new experiments lead to the same results, within fixed upper and lower limits. Subjective, and even intersubjective, experiences can give the same result with several observations, but they can also give different results. Today, we have several intersubjective perceptions about the consumption of various foods with regard to how beneficial or harmful they are for our health. In some regions, it is believed that cod liver oil is healthy for the heart. However, a large meta-survey of 68,000 people found that cod liver oil is neither good nor bad for the heart (Bunge, 2013: 130). On the other hand, it is good for those who produce this cod liver oil, they make a lot of money because specific cultural knowledge dictates that you should take cod liver oil because it is good for your cardiovascular health. In other words, one might say ironically that the only hearts that benefit from people taking cod liver oil are the hearts of those who make large profits from its sale. Of course, it is also possible that cod liver oil was originally used by people who needed extra fat, in order to cope with arduous work in harsh climatic conditions in regions where cod liver oil was readily available. For these people, the extra fat from cod liver oil would of course be good for both their heart and the rest of their body. In other words, there are many reasons why a belief that once served a purpose survives as a cultural "fact," and still exists. The point is though that intersubjectivity needs to be checked by using scientific trials to clarify the correctness of what is considered to be culturally produced "knowledge."

Meta-analyses are important for collecting knowledge that has been developed from several research projects. In contrast, few if any meta-analyses say anything about the mechanisms that result in the knowledge they produce. In order to prescribe the appropriate medical interventions, it is necessary to identify the causal mechanisms. This is where medical trials have an advantage. By trial and error, one can identify various mechanisms, for example, on a biological level in relation to the development path of a disease. Through trial and error, we know that we will sometimes fail. On the other hand, we also know that errors can lead to results that can be innovative in areas other than the problem being investigated. Even failed medical experiments can lead to the discovery of new knowledge and inventions, such as the discovery of penicillin.

Faith can move mountains, they say. On the other hand, mountains can separate people and beliefs. In our context, acupuncture, bloodletting for the treatment of pneumonia, homoeopathy, exorcism, and other religious rituals throughout the ages can result in personal and interpersonal experiences of people being cured of a disease or ailment; on the other hand, one can also say this was due to the placebo effect. It is only when scientific trials show that the aforementioned treatments have no real effect that new knowledge can be developed, and that "mountains" of new knowledge can begin to change beliefs.

MEDICAL ETHICS

Medical ethics have a direct impact on medical practice. Medical ethics can be said to be related to all the measures that promote an individual's well-being in hospitals, clinics, and all the places where people's health is in focus. Medical ethics are also important when examining unethical practices in the pharmaceutical industry, such as unethical experiments, or selling products at a higher price to developing countries than to industrialized countries. This can occur because developing countries often have weaker negotiating capacity than industrialized countries. Medical ethics is thus not something abstract and distant from ordinary people's lives; people can be directly or indirectly affected by the actions of the pharmaceutical industry in particular, and the health industry in general.

Medical ethics also comes into focus when new medicines are used in clinical trials involving animals before beginning clinical trials with people. Ethical concerns are often raised when the poor or economically disadvantaged are exploited in clinical research. In addition, the pricing of the products that have been subjected to such medical trials will also come under ethical scrutiny. To a large extent, the prices of many of the medicines produced by the large pharmaceutical companies are too high for people in poor countries. Moreover, there is little funding available for research into diseases that people in many developing countries suffer from, such as malaria, dengue fever, yellow fever, leprosy, and sleeping sickness (Bunge, 2013: 204).

Medical ethics are mainly applied to health systems and to a lesser degree outside the boundary of health systems. Why is this problematic? Let's take an example. If one finds by using scientific methods that great economic inequality leads to poorer health and more diseases amongst the economically disadvantaged, will such a discovery lead to a medical ethical debate? The answer is quite simple. Medical ethics mainly operates in relation to health systems and not outside these systems. This applies even if one can say with certainty that poverty and great economic inequality lead to the development of specific diseases in the poorer part of the population. On the basis of the above, one can propose the following hypothesis: Poverty causes disease and increases the dangers to health. If this hypothesis is correct, which it very likely is, then the question is the following? Will medical ethics be brought into the debate concerning the relationship between people's health and economic inequality?

In medical ethics, there are both norms and rules that apply. These change over time, while some remain long after they cease to have any function. Norms change more slowly than the rules. Therefore, you can often see that people's normative behaviour lasts longer than there is a basis for. This applies in the social system and also in the medical system. One of the consequences of the slow-moving course of history regarding medical norms is that some medical norms remain despite their lack of usefulness in the present. One example here is bloodletting as a treatment for various diseases long after it was scientifically proved that this did not lead to improvement for the patient. The norm persisted and made it more difficult to develop medical practice based on scientific knowledge. Moreover, the research around the benefits of acupuncture is lacking, as it is for other medical practices that still persist. While medical practice has been largely regulated in most countries, this does not apply to medical ethics to the same extent. If medical ethics is not closely linked to the scientific knowledge that is being developed, then we will probably see many strange developments in the future regarding medical practices.

We have compiled the above description in a conceptual model.

Analysis related to medical philosophy

Which health problems are real? How can we know if health problems are real and not socially constructed for a political purpose? These are two questions that need further investigation before it can be said that various problems in the healthcare sector exist. In philosophical terms, the two questions above are related to ontology and epistemology, respectively. Whether a health problem is real or not will be conditioned by who you ask, and in which historical and social context you ask the question. It can also be the case that someone's idea of what constitutes health can serve their interests. For instance, it is conceivable that large pharmaceutical companies have an interest in drawing attention to certain health problems instead of others, because they produce drugs that can treat the problem being focused on. However, it does not have to be the case that this health problem is the most important challenge people are facing. In this way, a certain way of thinking can influence people's perception of what constitutes a real health problem, and how this knowledge becomes part of people's consciousness.

From a knowledge perspective, we know that there is no direct causal connection between a situation, a condition, etc. and how one perceives this condition. To a large extent, there is a dialectical relationship between a condition that has been experienced or learned, and the knowledge one develops about this condition. In philosophical terms, what we know is conditioned by how we came to know it. The relationship between what seems real and the knowledge we have about a phenomenon, condition etc. is not a mechanical causal relationship, but a dialectical or interactive relationship. This is not an abstract idea, but an insight that has direct implications for practice. Let's take a concrete example. If a leader believes that there is a linear/mechanistic causal relationship between a company's working environment and the company's performance, then he/she will have established a model, which will also then serve as a starting point for any actions that are carried out. If a leader adopts such a model, then he/she will seek to improve the working environment, because he/she believes this will improve the company's performance. There is nothing wrong with this model, but it is thinkable that one can also adopt other models that are just as viable or even more viable. For instance, another leader may adopt a different model. This new leader views the relationship between the working environment and the performance of a company in a slightly more complicated way. He/she agrees that the working environment affects performance, but that this is only half the truth. The other part of the truth is, as this leader sees it, that performance also affects the working environment. This leader then has a different model than the first leader. The new leader can then influence performance by investing in new technology so that productivity and performance are improved. When performance is improved using this model, the working environment is also improved. When the working environment improves, this will have a positive effect on performance. It is not the case that one model is more "real" or "true" than the other, but they are just two different perceptions of reality. On the other hand, the leader who adopts the second more complex model will have a greater scope of action than the leader who adopted the first mechanistic/linear model.

The linear model is often used in the natural sciences and is based on linear causality, i.e., a simple type of causal relationship between events, usually involving a single cause that produces a single effect. The second model is based on systemic thinking or cybernetic thinking, which is an analytical approach to comprehending how different elements interact within a system, such as a social system. In other words, this concerns mainly circular or interactive processes which are rarely or never linear processes. In this way, systemic philosophy can help us understand, explain, and solve practical challenges related to social systems, including health systems.

On the basis of the above reflection, we can suggest the following proposition:

Proposition: What we perceive as "real" is largely determined by the knowledge model we have about a situation or event.

Practical implication: The greater the variety one has in one's knowledge models, the greater the probability of improved understanding and thus scope of action.

Theoretical reflections related to medical philosophy

The relationship between society and technology can have strong or weak links. At the same time, there can be little or great emphasis given to empirical data. It is the combination of these two dimensions that says something about how we can expect the health systems to function in the future.

Technology's increasing importance for production, distribution, and consumption creates major challenges and opportunities for most social systems, including health systems. The more integrated the global world is through information systems and opportunities for communication, the greater the likelihood that our health systems will be affected in one way or another by this development. It is the degree of connection between new technology and health systems that provides guidance for the challenges, problems, and opportunities we will see in the future. One can assume with a relatively high degree of certainty that there will be a greater degree of interconnection or integration between the physical world and the virtual world, as new technology becomes connected to the global information and communication networks. In practice, this may mean that specialists within certain medical fields, such as cancer treatment and cardiovascular disease, will be able to contribute to medical interventions on patients who are physically located in other parts of the world. This integration, where the virtual and the physical are integrated into practical actions, could revolutionize treatment methods, diagnoses, and the development of most health systems around the world. There are of course many ethical problems that will arise when this potentiality becomes an actual possibility. We will not discuss these ethical issues here but only note that they are serious, numerous, and not easy to find solutions to (Johannessen, 2021).

When this opportunity, regarding the integration of technological solutions, becomes realized, this will require that the empirical data used can be trusted. To exemplify such a development, one can imagine a situation where the virtual world and the physical world are fully integrated. For example, in the future when VR technologies are applied in surgery, when a surgeon located say, in Beijing, can carry out surgery on a patient located in Stockholm. Using VR technology the specialist in Beijing will be able to directly observe and perform surgery in real time in Stockholm with the cooperation of a team of health professionals and technicians located in Stockholm. The specialist in Beijing will receive continuous feedback using the VR technology, making it possible to carry out the operation remotely. This would be an example of a strong link between society and technology, as shown in Figure 4.2.

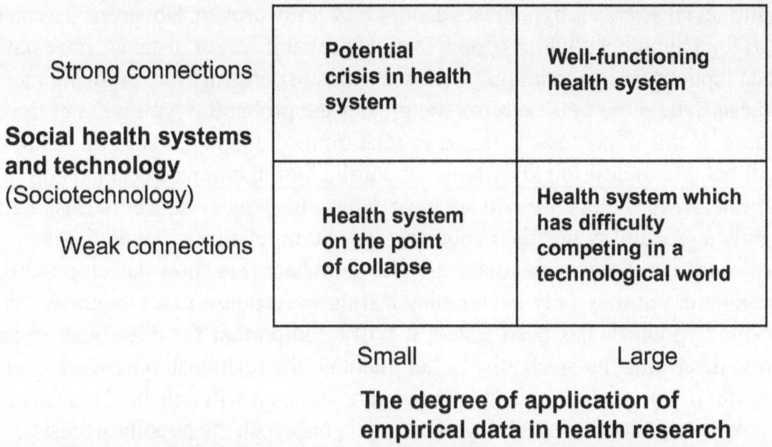

Figure 4.2 The relationships between sociotechnology and empirical data.

The scenario above regarding a strong link between society and technology will not be radically different from the media world of today, where we can observe in real time what is happening in a completely different place in the world. The only new aspect is that, in our example, it is possible to use the new and strong information and communication networks to connect technologies over large distances. To achieve this will require strong links between society and technology on the one hand, and a great trust in, and emphasis on, empirical data, on the other. It is when these two dimensions are linked that we can say that we have a systemic link that will be able to solve many of the challenges we have today in our health systems. The example we have used above of the Beijing surgeon and the patient in Stockholm is only meant to emphasize the point regarding future developments. For example, it can be imagined in the future that rural areas, where there is a shortage of medical expertise, will be able to access this expertise remotely. In practice, such a development will mean that there will be no need for specialists to move to rural areas, so that the population in these areas can receive specialist treatment.

In the global world, we have reached a point where technology and information systems have become a social mechanism for the development of our health systems. One can imagine that in a relatively short time, around 2030–2040, artificial intelligence and intelligent nano-sized robots will be able to be integrated into networks (Kurzweil, 2005; 2008; 2013). When this occurs, society and technology will have become very strongly linked.

The increasing link between society and technology via artificial intelligence and intelligent robots also promotes new ways of collecting and applying empirical data. In this context, we must be aware of the distinction between data and scientific evidence. Data only becomes scientific evidence in response to a hypothesis. Therefore, it is crucial to learn how to develop different forms of hypotheses, as well as the methods that can test these hypotheses against data.

In the social sciences, hypotheses cannot be wholly proven. However, we can find support for a hypothesis with a certain level of probability. For instance, if we have as our data input "physical training," we can use this to construct the following medical hypothesis: The more you exercise, the greater the probability you will not develop an illness. If this hypothesis is tested in relation to different types of diseases, then we will be able to develop knowledge about the aforementioned relationship in the hypothesis. Nevertheless, we will not have determined any evidence for this relationship, only a probability that the hypothesis is valid in relation to some diseases, such as cardiovascular diseases and diabetes. The point here is to show that empirical data are important, but they only become interesting in response to a hypothesis. When the above hypothesis has been tested, it will be important for those who research health to determine the mechanisms that maintain the relationship between exercise and health. If you don't do this, the knowledge you gain will only be descriptive and won't really explain the underlying phenomena on which the hypothesis rests.

There is a distinction in the subject literature between low-level and high-level hypotheses. A low-level hypothesis only contains concepts that can be found directly in the source data. A high-level hypothesis has at least one concept linked to it that cannot be found directly in the source data. In all cases, it will be impossible to formulate a low-level hypothesis, unless a high-level hypothesis already exists. Many of the most interesting results in recent research (e.g. quantum theory and chaos theory) did not emerge from source data. Instead, the motivation for their development was the lack of existing theories to explain factual findings.

It is possible to mechanize (automate) induction with the assistance of software programs, e.g., linear regression. But we must always be clear that the resulting hypotheses are only low-level hypotheses, and accordingly are of little theoretical interest. The generation of insightful high-level hypotheses is beyond the scope of any algorithm or software program. What one can do with a computer is to check whether a specific high-level hypothesis is compatible with a specific set of source data. In brief, computers can help us to process data and generate low-level hypotheses and to find out how well or poorly these fit with the data. But they can never be used to create high-level hypotheses, because these, by definition involve concepts that are not found in the source data. This is one of the reasons why theory development is important.

Merton (1967: 1–171) makes the following suggestions for theory-building processes:

1. Start with a simple idea, or an analogy.
2. The idea or the analogy will then provide the basis for the development of some simple postulates.
3. The idea, the analogy, and the postulates will provide the basis for the development of propositions and hypotheses, which can then be subjected to empirical testing.
4. The idea, or the analogy itself, will be tested for its effectiveness in the case of those theoretical problems and hypotheses that provoke us to examine new aspects of the phenomenon or problem.

We have reflected on theoretical assumptions related to the development of hypotheses, and systems of hypotheses. In Figure 4.2 we have compiled the reflections related to how medical philosophy, from a systemic perspective, can help us understand, explain, and solve some of the future health challenges.

We have derived the following propositions from Figure 4.2:

Proposition 1: The stronger the links that exist between social health systems and technology, and the greater the degree of application of empirical data in health research, the greater the probability of a well-functioning health system, because both technology and data are an integral part of health systems.

Proposition 2: The weaker the links that exist between social health systems and technology, and the greater the degree of application of empirical data in health research, the greater the likelihood that health systems will have problems competing in a technological world, because of the lack of integration of technology inhibits competition.

Proposition 3: The weaker the links that exist between social health systems and technology, and the smaller the degree of application of empirical data in health research, the greater the probability that the health systems will be on the point of collapse, because both the research and the use of technology will be harmed by such structuring.

Proposition 4: The stronger the links that exist between social health systems and technology, and the smaller the degree of application of empirical data in health research, the greater the probability that a potential crisis will develop in health systems, because the development of research will not be fact-based.

Practical utility related to medical philosophy

Trust and confidence are key components of healthcare. However, it takes a long time to build trust; however, trust can be broken by a single incident of poor treatment. It is in such situations that distrust begins to grow, where people develop lack of trust and confidence in healthcare. It is possible that increased use of new technology can improve trust. New technology, such as AI, can be used to gather and share information about health more efficiently. This spread of information can remedy the lack of information many people have about health systems. Amongst other things, information and knowledge strengthen the understanding and explanation of what happens in health systems. For instance, this could concern the course of disease progression of a patient, and why events occur that should not have occurred. The lack of information can breed rumours and gossip and result in unwanted situations arising, where people can lose their trust in healthcare. Against this background, new technology that can facilitate an improved dissemination of knowledge will counter such developments.

We can choose to look at health systems as a social construction. By this we do not mean that there are no objective facts that can be checked. Many of the physical and architectural designs in health systems and the physical technology that is used can be understood as objective elements. However, the thinking of the various professional groups in health systems is highly subjective. In other words, opinions, thoughts, and ideas are largely subjective. The dialectical relationship between the objective elements and the subjective ideas creates the reality that exists in healthcare systems. It does not need to be a problem that objective facts and subjective ideas flow into each other in health systems. In fact, subjective ideas when applied in practical situations can become objective in their consequences. This can be exemplified by a nurse's tacit knowledge, which is often referred to as the "clinical gaze." The clinical gaze is a subjective quantity. It is difficult to transfer this tacit knowledge as information from those who have this knowledge to those who do not (Johannessen, 2022). It is also difficult, almost impossible, to reflect on this type of knowledge between the people who have this knowledge and those who do not. It can be said that the clinical gaze grows out of long experience. A novice works according to a set of rules and he/she evaluates his/her work in terms of how well it follows the rules. Gradually, these rules become routine. When this routine is followed over a period of time the nurse will gradually begin to acquire tacit knowledge. This tacit knowledge, or "clinical gaze," can be defined as the skills and experiences the nurse has acquired, but which cannot be easily expressed verbally or codified. In other words, this knowledge cannot be digitized and transferred via any technological network. On the other hand, when this knowledge is applied in practical contexts, it will be possible to observe the results. In this context, one might say that the "clinical gaze" is subjective, but objective when applied in practice.

With this example, we have exemplified how healthcare is a social construction that manifests itself in the borderland between the subjective and the objective. In this context, the following question can be formulated: How can subjective ideas in a health system become objective realities? This question has been addressed by Berger and Luckmann (1966: 30) in their classic book, *The Social Construction of Reality*. In a hospital various human activities create both subjective perceptions and objective realities. This is a dialectical process. It is in this context that we say that healthcare is a social construction. It is precisely when this social construction utilizes new AI technology that we can tackle this process in a more adequate way. It is imaginable that generative artificial intelligence will contribute to bridging the gap between the subjective and the objective, for example in a hospital, i.e., between subjective perceptions and objective realities.

Carrying out medical trials promotes medical development. With the introduction of artificial intelligence and robotics it will be possible to virtually conduct medical trials; these can be simulated thousands of times using learning algorithms. Empirical data can be generated and tested virtually, so that humans do not have to be used as guinea pigs. Such experiments will develop insights into medical regularities, which in turn can create medical laws. Development of this technology will promote medical research and will enable making quantum leaps in tackling many of the diseases that have become more prevalent in urban centres, such asdealing with zoonotic diseases which are caused by germs that spread between animals and people in close contact with each other.

A negative aspect of increased urbanization and movements of people and animals is that diseases that previously only existed in animals have now become more common amongst humans, such as monkeypox, AIDS, SARS, COVID-19, and so on (Diamond, 1997: 206); these diseases have had a severe effect on human health. In this regard, one can develop the following proposition: The greater the rate of urbanization in the future, the greater will be the need to use AI systems in research to predict disease development and find cures. In other words, this need will arise with increased urbanization, when more and more people come into contact with each other, also across national borders. Thus, accelerating migration and urbanization will increase the danger of zoonotic diseases, i.e., diseases caused by germs that spread between animals and people. This became evident with the rapid spread of COVID-19 in 2020–2022. We have little experience with these types of diseases and have therefore become more vulnerable to epidemics and pandemics. In this context, we don't have time to carry out the classic experiments by first testing on animals and then conducting controlled experiments with humans. We need to find methods that greatly reduce the time from when a disease is discovered until a cure is developed. This is where virtual experiments, and the generation of data from learning algorithms, can be of help. If we can also develop generative artificial intelligence that can create syntheses of this "empirical" data, then we will also be able to develop medical applications to deal with future communicable diseases.

Apart from the increase in zoonotic diseases, increased urbanization, poor sanitation, and poor waste management have also increased the risk of other types of diseases, such as tuberculosis, dengue, and diarrhoea. In addition, climate change and rising temperatures are also negatively affecting people's health in various ways.

Another consequence of increasing urbanization and the way we live today is that we have become increasingly dependent on people we do not know and who we know nothing about. This has resulted, in some cases, in the development of new types of diseases and mental illnesses. Stressful urban living can trigger or aggravate some mental disorders in some people. If we know that we are dependent on people whom we are not able to trust, how will this affect us? At one level or another we depend on others. Humans have been dependent on each other since pre-historic times when they roamed across the African savannah in small groups. The point is that these humans knew those whom they depended on. In today's big cities, and civilizations based on these big cities, we barely know those who live next door or other people we depend on for our survival. Not knowing or trusting the people you depend on can put people's mental health at risk. Some people are unable to tackle such a situation, and this uncertainty can lead to stress, angst, and mental challenges. Of course, it's not the case that we go around thinking that we are dependent on people we don't know. The point in this context is that on a historical level, in our consciousness, we know from the time when we roamed in

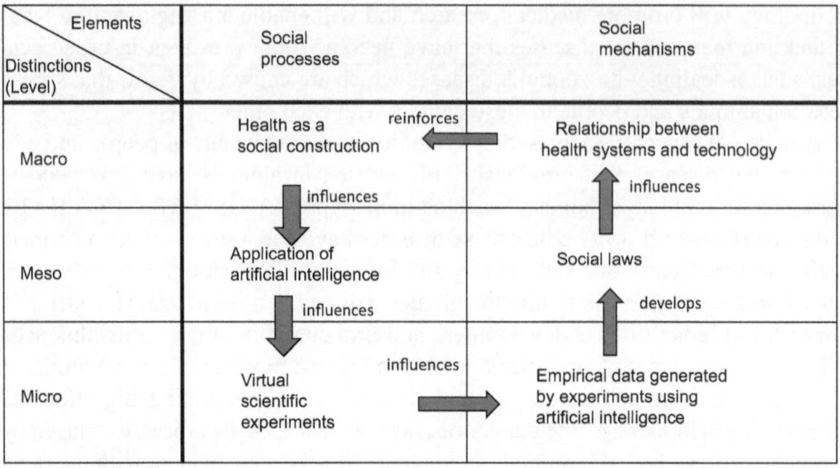

Figure 4.3 Medical philosophy: A Boudon–Coleman diagram.

small groups across the African savannah that we are literally dependent on others for our survival. This historical consciousness can play tricks on us and make us ill when we realize both unconsciously and consciously that we are dependent on others, but we do not know those we are dependent on.

On a slightly absurd level, we can say that we create our own illnesses by remembering at a historically deep level our dependence on others. These others rule over our lives without us knowing who they are. The others don't know who we are either. Thus, this mutual dependence can also become a factor that reinforces mental disorders. When the pain of these mental disorders becomes too great, some people believe that mental illness is punishment from God. Of course, in reality, it is punishment we have inflicted on ourselves by the way we organize our lives. If we believe that our mental pain is a punishment from God then one can say that we are maintaining the pain, so that it becomes a depressive illness. In this way, it might be said, that, in many instances, there is a link between strong religious belief, pain, and depression (Bunge, 2013: 51).

We have compiled the reflections in this section in a Boudon–Coleman diagram (Figure 4.3).

Conclusion

The following question has been examined: How can the philosophy of medicine, viewed from a systemic perspective, help us to understand, explain, and resolve some of the future challenges in the healthcare sector? In contemporary society, the field of medicine is characterized by strong links between medical science, medical practice, and medical technology. These links are evident in the health industry, the pharmaceutical industry, and the university hospitals, where various forms of medical knowledge are tested.

Modern medical knowledge is no longer based on subjective ideas, religious and cultural beliefs, shaman practices, and so on. Amongst other things, medical knowledge today concerns knowledge of various diseases, and the established and evolving biomedical, clinical, and epidemiological sciences, as well as the scientific application of this knowledge to patients. The scientific methods used are largely taken from the fields of biology, physics, and chemistry, and the social sciences and historical methods. In this way, medical research has moved from the subjective, religious, and cultural fields to the scientific field. It can be said that medical competence lies at the intersection between technology, natural sciences, and applied sciences. Medical science is multidisciplinary. It gathers knowledge from several other disciplines, such as pharmacology, biophysics, biochemistry, bioengineering, nanotechnology, molecular biology, genetics, cytology, neuroscience, immunology, bacteriology, parasitology, toxicology, physiotherapy, hospital management, ethics, scientific theory, sociology, history, etc.

It is important to be aware of the relationship between applied medical sciences and medical expertise. For example, surgery is a branch of medical science where surgeons with medical expertise treat illnesses or injuries by operative procedures. The same is true of pharmacology. A pharmacist has medical expertise about how drugs interact with the body, but he/she also specializes in the practical application, design, and administration of medication.

Medical knowledge is consistently articulated in relation to the diagnosis and treatment of disease. Physicians diagnose and treat illnesses, and prescribe medications, in collaboration with pharmacists, while nurses promote health and help patients with illnesses. In other words, the expertise and knowledge of these professional groups are centred around the diagnosis and treatment of disease. Medical knowledge is also related to and dependent upon scientific fields, such as biochemistry, biophysics, sociology, and so on. Although medical knowledge is dependent on knowledge from these scientific fields, health can, from certain perspectives, be viewed as a social construct, as health is often defined and assessed differently by different people.

Is malnutrition a disease or a condition that can lead to various forms of disease? Should medical research be interested in malnutrition or in the diseases that can result from malnutrition? Should medical expertise be concerned with both malnutrition and the diseases that can be the result of malnutrition? Is malnutrition a disease in the medical sense, or is it the result of social processes outside the focus area of medical knowledge? These questions are important for the focus area of medicine and medical research.

Healthcare is increasingly embracing and adopting new technology. This is increasing complexity in both hospitals and other health organizations. Health professionals who work in these health organizations often need to have both medical and technological expertise. The hospital treatment of patients today, and more so in the future, often concerns the involvement of many professionals, the so-called multidisciplinary teams, where professionals have both medical and technological expertise. Communication within such teams is important in order to provide patients with comprehensive care. In other words, the members of such teams need to develop their communication, relationship, and social skills. Consequently, this development is also leading to increasing complexity in health organizations.

Medical research involves research in various fields with the goal of developing new medicines and treatments. Medical research utilizes empirical data and medical trials, with the aim of establishing the safe, effective, and practical application of treatments, medications, and so on.

Medical trials need to be based on ethical principles and values, e.g., when collecting empirical data. Medical ethics sets limits for what can and cannot be allowed when conducting medical research. Effective and quality healthcare, in hospitals and other health organizations, often requires the involvement of many health professionals with different skills. On the other hand, it might be said that nurses are the backbone of healthcare, providing care for patients. Nurses possess medical expertise in relation to recognizing patients' symptoms, administering medications, and so on, but they also take care of patients' comfort. If we consider hospitals metaphorically as a living organism then it is the nurses who keep this organism together, so that it can function as a unit.

An important philosophical point regarding the competence of nurses is that they have competence and knowledge of how patients are treated throughout the course of an illness. Philosophically, this is the knowledge that goes by the name of know-how, in contrast to doctors' know-what. This knowledge is developed through experience and often goes by the name of tacit knowledge or "clinical gaze." It was the philosophers Bertrand Russell and Michael Polanyi (1966; 1969) who first reflected on these different types of knowledge. Bertrand Russell distinguished between know-what and know-how (Bunge, 2013). Polanyi (2015) distinguished between tacit knowledge and explicit knowledge. In this way, it can be said that there is a link between philosophy and the medical understanding and practical explanation of a nurse's knowledge and competence.

Medicine involves skills that are recognized as scientific as well as the practical application of medical procedures. As a science, medicine is based on empiricism, scientifically recognized methods, and the development of knowledge based on objective and verifiable experiments. As a practical skill, medicine is based on the application of treatments and procedures. This often involves the so-called tacit knowledge, which is knowledge that is not objective in the scientific sense. However, the exercise of tacit knowledge is objective and verifiable in that it is measurable in its consequences. On this basis, this is in disagreement with Bunge who expressed that "gut feeling" is in opposition to science (Bunge, 2013: 211). As mentioned, tacit knowledge may be considered "scientific" in its consequences (Johannessen, 2022). Claiming that tacit knowledge is not scientific, in the sense that it is not theoretical, is like saying that those who apply this type of knowledge follow non-scientific practices. Such a claim undermines the skills and knowledge of nurses, whose work is often based on tacit knowledge. On the other hand, medicine is not only concerned with expertise, which Dreyfus and Dreyfus (1980) claim, but also involves competencies that can be defined as a system of knowledge, skills, and attitudes (Johannessen, 2022).

Knowledge and skills are systemically linked, rather than by a linear causal relationship. You can develop skills and thus build up experiences that turn into knowledge over time, e.g., tacit knowledge. On the other hand, one can develop knowledge, e.g., explicit knowledge, which can be turned into skills through various practical processes, e.g., the surgeon's theoretical knowledge of anatomy and then the exercise of this theoretical knowledge in learning processes, either on human cadavers or animals, or using current technology, through virtual practical exercises.

When Bunge (2013) claims that teaching nurses to develop theories is like the "inventiveness of adventures," then we completely disagree with this claim and this view of knowledge. Bunge (1974: v) has defined a theory as "a system of propositions." You can of course learn to develop such propositions through practice and then systematize this practice in typologies. Then, in a typology, you will be able to develop four propositions, which in their consequences can be understood as a mini-theory; you can also claim that mini-theories can be important.

Notes

1 https://www.newstatesman.com/spotlight/2022/02/why-now-is-the-time-to-propel-healthcare-into-the-next-era
2 https://www.newstatesman.com/spotlight/2022/02/why-now-is-the-time-to-propel-healthcare-into-the-next-era
3 Represented by, among others, Suppe (1977), Sneed (1976; 1979), Von Fraasen (1980), and Stegmyller (1979).

References

Baird, F. (2023). *Philosophic classics: From Plato to Derrida*, Routledge, London.
Bateson, G. (1972). *Steps to an ecology of mind*, Intex Books, New York.
Berger, P. & Luckmann, T. (1966). *The social construction of reality*, Allen Lane, London.
Bunge, M. (1974). *Sense and reference*, Reidel, Dordrecht.
Bunge, M. (1983). *Understanding the world*, Reidel, Dordrecht.
Bunge, M. (1989). *Treatise on basic philosophy, ethics: The good and the right*, vol. 8, Reidel, Dordrecht.
Bunge, M. (1996). *Finding philosophy in social science*, Yale University Press, New Haven.
Bunge, M. (1998). *Social science under debate*, University of Toronto Press, Toronto.
Bunge, M. (2001). *Scientific realism*, Prometheus, New York.
Bunge, M. (2013). *Medical philosophy: Conceptual issues in Medicine*, WSPC, London.
Diamond, J. (1997). *Guns, germs, and steel*, W.W. Norton, New York.
Dreyfus, S.A. & Dreyfus, H.L. (1980). *A five stage model of the mental activities involved in directed skill acquisition*, Storming Media, Washington, DC.
Habermas, J. (1968). *Knowledge and human interests*, Beacon, Boston.
Johannessen, J-A. (2021). *Artificial intelligence, automation and ethics in the innovation economy*, Routledge, London.
Johannessen, J-A. (2022). *The philosophy of tacit knowledge*, Emerald, London.
Kuhn, T. (1976). *The structure of scientific revolutions*, Chicago University Press, Chicago.
Kurzweil, R. (2005). *The singularity is near*, Penguin, London.
Kurzweil, R. (2008). *The age of spiritual machines: When computers exceed human intelligence*, Penguin, London.

Kurzweil, R. (2013). *How to create a mind: The secret of human thought revealed*, Penguin Books, New York.
Merton, R.K. (1967). *Social theory and social structure*, Free Press, London.
Polanyi, M. (1966). *The tacit dimension*, Doubleday, New York.
Polanyi, M. (1969). *Knowing and being*, University of Chicago Press, Chicago.
Polanyi, M. (2015). *Personal knowledge*, University of Chicago Press, Chicago.
Sneed, J.D. (1976). *Philosophical problems in the empirical science: a formal approach erkenntnis*, 10, 115–146.
Sneed, J.D.(1979). *The logical structure of mathematical physics*, Reidel, Dordrecht.
Stegmyller, W. (1979). *The structuralist view of theories: A possible analogue of the Boubaki Programme in physical science*, Springer, Berlin.
Suppe, P. (1977). *The structure of scientific discovery*, University of Illinois Press, Urbana.
Turner, J. (1991). *The structure of sociological theory*, Wadsworth Publishing Company, Belmont.
Urmson, J.O. & Ree, J. (eds.). (1989). *The concise encyclopaedia of western philosophy and philosophers*, Unwin Hyman, London.
Von Fraassen, B.C. (1980). *The scientific image*, Clarendon Press, Oxford.
Von Wright, G.H. (1971). *Explanation and understanding*, Cornell University Press, New York.

Part II

Disability and inclusion in working life

An important purpose of Part II is to show how we can develop a socially inclusive environment for everyone in working life, both those with disabilities and others. Another purpose is to find the social mechanisms that create and maintain social exclusion in working life, regarding people with disabilities.

The motivation for writing this part is linked to the following assumption. Paradoxically, the new technology will very likely be of help in working life for people with disabilities. In the future, the new technology will be of great help to the blind and partially sighted, for example in the utilization of GPS (Renda & Kuys, 2013). On the other hand, the new technology will increase automation and digitalization, and be more focused on efficiency and productivity. Technology will thus, on the one hand, facilitate the social inclusion of people with disabilities, but also perhaps lead to social exclusion due to the focus on productivity. This paradox can be termed technological serendipity, because new technology has within it the possibility of social inclusion due to the development of events by chance in a beneficial way. However, technological advances may also result in social exclusion. In other words, it is often quite random and entirely up to individual organizations whether or not new technology results in the inclusion or exclusion of people with disabilities.

The problem we are addressing concerns how the new technology can expand or restrict the functional range of people with disabilities in working life. In this context, we will focus on two different perspectives. The first perspective focuses on high-tech, where technology makes everything possible, including for people with disabilities. We term the second perspective, a social-deterministic perspective. In this perspective, it is assumed that people with disabilities do not have a future in the new working life, where technology will dominate. In this part, we adopt a perspective that balances the two contrasting perspectives.

Put bluntly, one can say that society creates an environment in the workplace, and in the system around the workplace, for example, transport to and from the workplace, which means that some of us develop special needs. These can be physical, mental, cognitive, or psychological needs. The employer then says that they cannot employ people with such needs, because it will harm the organization's

DOI: 10.4324/9781003497325-6

productivity. When it is imagined that someone does not promote this productivity, then you can say that you have no use for such people. In this context, a Danish saying seems appropriate: “First they piss on us, then they tell us that we stink.” Also in this context, a sign at an English airport says: “Not all disabilities are visible.” This is also something that people should take note of.

5 AI, robotics, and the social inclusion of people with disabilities in the workplace

Key points

- **Technological serendipity**: New technology has within it the possibility of social inclusion due to the development of events by chance in a beneficial way. However, technological advances may also result in social exclusion.
- **Fear of diversity**: If diversity stimulates creativity and innovation, and these are the main social mechanisms if organizations are to succeed in the Fourth Industrial Revolution (FIR), then it is the people who fear diversity who pose the largest problem for the progress of organizations, institutions, and other social systems.
- **"Model power"**: The models we use to understand and explain social phenomena create attitudes, which then trigger actions. On the other hand, actions can also change attitudes and create new models.
- **New technology can help people with disabilities**: New technology, such as AI and robotics, can diminish or eliminate some of the barriers faced by people with disabilities in working life and create new opportunities.
- **Human augmentation technology**: In the Fourth Industrial Revolution, new human augmentation technology will most probably represent a major technological breakthrough for people with disabilities.
- **"Minority body"**: Physically disabled people and people with special needs can be said to have a "minority body," and are often dependent on the development of new technological innovations.

Introduction

In this chapter, we will base our discussion on what is termed "the creating capabilities approach" or the "human development approach" (Nussbaum, 2011).[1]

If a country's gross national product increases every year, but also the number of its people deprived of basic education, healthcare, and other opportunities, is that country really making progress in terms of people's well-being? This is the question asked by Martha Nussbaum in her book, *Creating Capabilities* (2011), which focuses on the life situations of people with disabilities. If economic growth is to be understood not only as an increase in GNP per capita, but also in relation to

DOI: 10.4324/9781003497325-7

people's well-being, then society needs to ensure that people with disabilities are treated equally with regard to social inclusion in working life.

One of the main challenges regarding people with disabilities is that employers and researchers have a tendency to homogenize them into a single group (Roulstone, 2016: 5). This approach tends to ignore the fact that people with special needs, or people with disabilities, have as many different needs as people without disabilities. The point here is that people with disabilities have some additional needs.

In this chapter, we use different knowledge perspectives to address the general research question. Our scientific theoretical approach is based on systemic thinking, as developed by the philosopher Mario Bunge.[2] We will refer to the fields of sociology, philosophy, ethics, innovation theory, knowledge management, and technology[3] when addressing the general research question and the research sub-questions. We are of the opinion that the new technology will be of decisive importance in promoting the well-being of people with disability challenges.

AI and robotics do not represent a threat to people with disabilities. On the contrary, this technology can help them gain access to the labour market. It is rather people's negative attitudes towards them that can result in lack of opportunities and work. In other words, the belief that everyone should be equally productive and useful to employers. Thus, the threat to people with disabilities is when people adopt a mindset based on social exclusion, and this becomes the dominant social mindset. This creates models and frameworks that result in people with disabilities being dependent on care, and thus marginalized and pushed out of the so-called efficient, rational, and productive working life.

There will always be some people who are more productive than others, and better at performing various work tasks, even if we do not include people with disabilities. On the other hand, it is not productivity that will be a challenge in the Fourth Industrial Revolution (FIR), because the increased development of AI and robotics will lead to increased productivity. It is the attitudes of people that are the real challenges for everyone, both those with disabilities and those who for one reason or another are less-productive than others. Our aim here is to investigate what motivates people and organizations to hire, or not hire, people with disabilities.

We need to recognize that we cannot be highly productive at all times, after all, we are not machines! Although each of us has varying levels of productivity, an organization, as a whole, will be able to maintain stable productivity. This will especially apply in an age where AI and robotics are being increasingly used.

In this chapter, we will examine the following general research question: *How can artificial intelligence and intelligent robots affect the employment of people with disabilities in organizations?*

In order to examine the general research question, we have formulated the following six research sub-questions. All the research questions focus on artificial intelligence and intelligent robots.

RQ1: How are people with disabilities discriminated against in working life?
RQ2: How can organizations be motivated to hire people with disabilities?
RQ3: How can different attitudes affect the employment of people with disabilities?

RQ4: How can different types of leadership influence the employment of people with disabilities?
RQ5: How can different types of working environment affect the employment of people with disabilities?
RQ6: How can innovation and productivity affect the employment of people with disabilities?

The general research question and the six research sub-questions will be first examined in this chapter. In Chapter 6, we will examine Question 1 in more detail, amongst other things.

Figure 5.1 shows a figurative description of the introduction. Figure 5.1 also shows how this chapter is organized.

A historical introduction to discrimination strategies

In this section, we will examine the following question: How are people with disabilities discriminated against in working life?

It is often assumed, historically speaking, that people with disabilities have always had problems being socially included and finding employment. However, according to several authors, this was not always the case. In the Greco-Roman world, disability and deformity were socially accepted (Garland, 2010: 178; Quarmby, 2011: 16). For example, just think of all the soldiers who were severely injured and crippled during the numerous wars. How could one expect to recruit soldiers, if injured soldiers were socially excluded? How can you expect people with disabilities, who are especially talented, to apply for work when the working

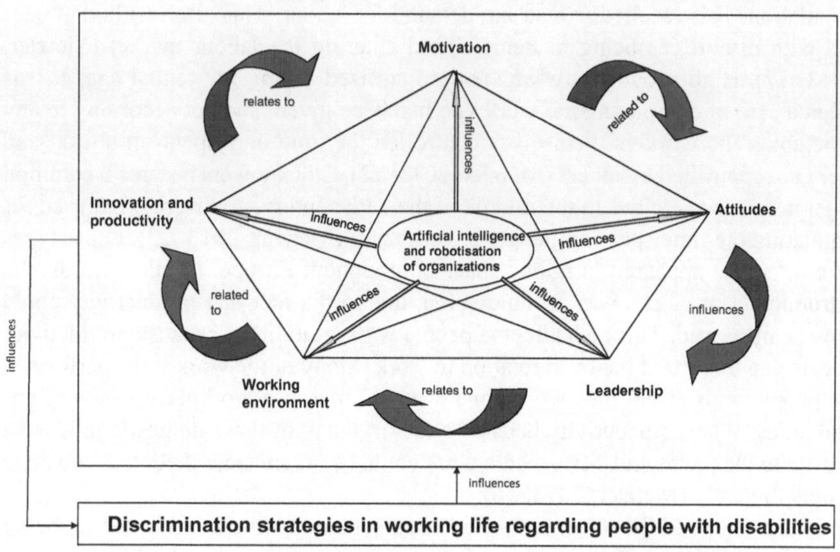

Figure 5.1 Intelligent robots and social inclusion in working life for people with disabilities.

environment does not fully accept them? Attitudes to disability have changed over time, the present perceptions often differ from past perceptions with regard to discrimination and social exclusion from working life. In ancient Egypt, physical disabilities were often considered as divine attributes given to humans by the gods. In ancient Greece (Rose, 2003)[4] and the Roman Empire (Laes et al., 2013; Laes, 2018), people with disabilities were not socially excluded or marginalized, but included in working life and the social community.

Different perceptions of people with disabilities throughout history

Feudal society

In feudal society, people with disabilities were often viewed as witches or evil beings (Metzler, 2006: 6). This superstition was reinforced by the Church which believed that these people were being punished for their own or their ancestors' sins[5] (Metzler, 2013).

The feudal lords were often not interested in new technology and new ways of organizing work, because this could easily lead to too much autonomy for the farm workers. This was one of the reasons why innovations spread very slowly in Europe, such as the heavy-wheeled plough and watermill (Slorach, 2016: 59). When the towns grew, they became a counterweight to the feudal lords' power. The trade carried out in the towns resulted in new laws and new professions, such as the clerks who could keep accounts of purchases and sales. In these jobs, people with certain disabilities were often hired for various reasons. We should keep in mind that the Catholic Church was the largest landowner in the Middle Ages, and was an important social mechanism in hindering the decline of feudal society.

The Black Death, other epidemics, and famine killed 50 per cent of Europe's population. This resulted in a strong demand for labour. This also resulted in people with disabilities being in demand and entering the labour market (Metzler, 2013: 77). High productivity was not emphasized during the feudal age. It was often a case of completing the work you had been given, and not according to any timetable. The workers themselves controlled the time they spent on a task, and were not controlled by others (Metzler, 2013: 72). Clock towers became a common sight in towns and cities in the middle of the 14th century, and were often used for regulating the time spent on people's work tasks (Metzler, 2013: 72). Other types of clocks also appeared in public spaces, throughout Europe. In other words, the introduction of clocks was an innovation, due to the fact that productivity could now be measured. This also affected people with disabilities, because productivity became an important factor in relation to work. Many of the work tasks performed by people with disabilities were done at home, not at a workplace in the towns and cities. When productivity became a factor, many of these domestic jobs were moved to the towns and cities where work could be organized, scheduled, and done more efficiently (Metzler, 2013: 76).

In the late Middle Ages, an "idiot" was someone who was viewed as being mentally deficient and incapable of ordinary reasoning (Goodey, 2011: 221). These "idiots" were also called fools, imbeciles, simpletons, and so on. Many royal courts throughout royal history employed the so-called "fools" for entertainment. However, these "fools," or court jesters, were not intellectually deficient but often highly intelligent. They merely played a role, in order to make a living. Apart from entertaining the court with humour, the "fool" often possessed insight and wisdom, and were able to expose the truth (Metzler, 2013: 86).

In the Middle Ages, it was believed that the intellect and soul were unified. It was not until the 17th to the 18th centuries, with the breakthrough of science, that people began to distinguish between permanent and temporary forms of mental illness, where people with temporary mental illness would nowadays be defined as the mentally ill (Goodey, 2011: 201–203).

At the end of the 17th century, poor relief legislation was introduced in England that required landowners to look after the poor and disabled, such as the mentally ill, the blind, and the lame (Harman, 2017: 175–204).

In feudal society, the serfs had some control over their working hours. They also had some control over production, and could use part of their agricultural production to feed themselves. Production and the home were not separated. The exploitation of the serfs was transparent. It was not difficult to see that the serfs were exploited in the feudal system. The hierarchy was explicit, and so was the oppression of the serfs. The serfs worked a certain period of time for the landowner, and it was quite clear that exploitation was taking place. In addition, the serf paid taxes to the landowner for the food that he produced.

The rise of capitalism in the 17th century

Modern capitalism is commonly believed to have started around the early 1600s, with the foundation of stock exchanges and joint-stock companies, first in the Netherlands, and then in Britain and France (Johannessen, 2018). The rise of capitalism resulted in an increased focus on efficiency, productivity, and profit, while excluding disabled people from equal participation in the labour force (Slorach, 2016: 42–58).

In the 16th and 18th centuries, Europe, and other parts of the world, were radically changed by the ideas of the Enlightenment, the emergence of capitalism, and the advent of the scientific revolution. The humanist ideals of the Enlightenment of the late 17th and 18th centuries emphasized reason and individualism as opposed to tradition. The emergence of capitalism eroded the social structures of feudal society, while the scientific revolution challenged the traditional beliefs of the Catholic Church.[6]

These economic, social, and cultural changes led to the strengthening of the bourgeoisie; during the course of the First Industrial Revolution a conflict emerged between the growing working class and the bourgeoisie (Harman, 2017).

Industrialization, which began around 1750 in Britain, resulted in a decline in the cottage industries, when production was increased by introducing industrial production in the factories. The disabled who worked in their homes, i.e., in the cottage industry, were now increasingly made redundant. In the factories, it was the most productive workers who were in demand. The growth of factories led to urbanization, as large numbers of people moved from rural areas to work in factories. In other words, industrial capitalism negatively impacted the disabled, at least in the short term. In the longer term, productivity increased and humanist ideals fostered by the working class, amongst others, led to increased care for the disabled, although not necessarily employment. It seems reasonable to argue that the first three industrial revolutions[7] increased the care for the disabled. However, it can also be said that during the First Industrial Revolution, people with disabilities were greatly discriminated against, because they were viewed as being unproductive in the industrial system (Stratford, 1989).

In addition to this, the poor working conditions in many industries, such as the railways, led to a great number of work-related accidents and injuries (Jacques-Stiker, 1982). When these workers could no longer work in the industry, they largely had to fend for themselves (Nielsen, 2012). On the one hand, people with disabilities were discriminated against regarding employment in industry. On the other hand, hundreds of thousands who were the victims of work-related accidents were pushed out of the labour market (Nielsen, 2012).

Industrial capitalism became the most dynamic and productive economic system viewed from a historical perspective. However, industrial capitalism, from 1750 onwards, largely excluded disabled people from participation in the labour force, as they were viewed as unproductive. This led to an institutionalization of disabled people and the so-called asylum system which consisted of institutions that provided asylum for the disabled (Campbell & Oliver, 2006). At the beginning of industrial capitalism around 1750, disabled people were still able to work from their homes as part of the cottage industry. According to Renda and Kuys (2013), this became more and more difficult as market forces took over and controlled the production conditions in factories and urban areas.

Industrialization and increased mechanization in factories replaced the craft workshops, because the factories were more productive. The craft workshops in the local communities often employed disabled people; these people were now excluded from the labour force. In other words, the new factory machines, and the new methods of production, placed new demands on the labour force, which the disabled were unable to meet; as a consequence, they were discriminated against in the labour market.

The factories and mines of the 19th century resulted in a great number of work-related injuries. Child labourers who worked in the coal mines often suffered serious physical injuries and they often developed serious diseases related to the work environment. Eventually, the hazardous working conditions of child labourers caused much social and political concern, resulting in the introduction of legislation aimed at improving conditions, prohibiting the employment of very young children, and limiting the number of hours worked (Borsay, 2005: 126). Towards the end of the 18th century, and during the 19th century, institutions were established for poor people without regular employment, and also people with physical and mental disabilities, who were also unable to work (Barnes, 1992). These were the so-called workhouses and asylums. The conditions in these workhouses and asylums were often so grotesque that new laws were adopted to improve conditions for the poor, the disabled, and the elderly in these institutions (Borsay, 2005: 22–30).

In the capitalist system, as opposed to the feudal system, the worker is paid wages for the work he/she carries out. The value-addition created by the worker was distributed as wages for the worker and profit for the capitalist. In this context, it might be said that people with disabilities are often incapable of creating value-addition that can be distributed as wages and profit. It might also be said that in the pre-industrial age, the value-addition created by disabled workers went wholly to the disabled worker as income. This can partly explain why during the period of industrial capitalism people with disabilities were not in demand due to their inability to provide profit to capital owners.

The Fourth Industrial Revolution and people with disabilities

It is a common assumption that people with disabilities need special accommodation at their workplace. This costs money and cuts into profits. Even with new technology, their productivity will be less than those without disabilities; at least this is what people assume (Barnes, 1992; Borsay, 2005). Based on a profit logic, the view is that people with disabilities are therefore a financial burden for organizations. Against this background, people with disabilities are seldom offered full-time work.

However, in the global economy, the value chain is being atomized and spread around the world according to a logic of cost, quality, competence, and innovation (Johannessen, 2018; 2018a); this development will most probably be reinforced in the Fourth Industrial Revolution. This will lead to a return to a form of "home production" that existed before industrialization. Of course, in practise this is not a return in real terms to this old form of production, but it is used here as a metaphor because it makes it easier to understand this new development. This "home production," in the Fourth Industrial Revolution, may lead to an increased demand for people with disabilities, because many of them have high skills, can focus on special work tasks, and also work on contracts from their home offices. The home office is not an extra cost for organizations, and the individual has already equipped their home with any special facilities they might need, which is an additional cost the employer does not have to pay for.

Sub-conclusion

The above description suggests that during the Fourth Industrial Revolution there may be an increase in demand in the labour market for people with disabilities. To what extent people will be hired as contract workers is uncertain. It is probable that competence and the quality of the delivery will be decisive in determining the income of those who work from their home offices, both for those with disabilities and those without disabilities. These contracts can apply to various types of production, such as clothing production, the production of computer parts, the production of vehicle components, and so on. This increase in home production may result in a decrease in factory production. The "home production" will most probably use AI applications and robotics in the production process. This future scenario would improve the opportunities for disabled people in the labour market.

The main hypothesis for the Fourth Industrial Revolution (FIR) is the following: FIR will lead to the inclusion of people with disabilities.

Explanation: A return to "home production."

Motivation

In this section, we will examine the following research question: How can organizations be motivated to hire people with disabilities? Increased competition to reduce costs in the global economy will, as a general rule, be a factor that demotivates leaders to employ people with disabilities. On the other hand, it can well be imagined that it is precisely this increasing competition, together with the new technology of the Fourth Industrial Revolution, which will open up new opportunities and motivate organizations to employ people with disabilities. Moreover, there is much research that focuses on the benefits of hiring people from disadvantaged groups. For example, maturity in people over a certain age often results in them being more creative (Hickson & Housley, 2006: 539–547); the ability of people with Asperger's Syndrome to focus on detail (Attwood, 2015), and the ability of people with dyslexia to be creative (Rooke, 2016; 2018).

By using intelligent robots to ease some of the incapacities people with disabilities have, the new technology can be a driver for employing these people. What initially seemed like an obstacle, disability, can, under the new technological conditions, be a motivating factor for hiring these people. The point is, then, that in some contexts it may be advantageous to hire people with disabilities.

Narratives related to motivation

Case letter 1: Creativity and older workers

It is often assumed that older workers are less creative than younger workers. At a time when creativity is an important social mechanism for promoting productivity in organizations, such an assumption can have major negative consequences for older workers. Is this assumption correct? Empirical research has shown that older employees are often more creative given that the work situation is controllable, but less creative otherwise (Binnewies et al., 2008). This knowledge can be used to increase creativity in certain contexts. This knowledge can also be used to organize work operations so that older employees work in environments that are controllable. In the same way, the research can be used to support younger workers, where there is a desire for increased creativity. For the younger workers, a better use of their creative potential is to place them in work situations where the work processes are not controllable.

If leaders are aware of what we have described above, then this should motivate them to organize work in such a way that they retain older workers for certain tasks where creativity is essential.

Case letter 2: ADHD is my superpower

Consider these three scenarios, all of which could materialize in the not-too-distant future, once robotics and artificial intelligence (AI) have become part of everyday life.

SCENARIO 1:

By taking a new drug, people with ADHD can work on a single problem for a prolonged period of time with levels of focus and energy that are far above normal. Such abilities are of particular interest to employers in need of people to supervise robotized production facilities. Our question is: Is it ethically acceptable to supply this drug to people with ADHD, so that they can achieve peak levels of productivity?

SCENARIO 2:

Factory A, which has an AI-facilitated production line, wants to recruit employees who won't be distracted by their social lives. Ideal candidates for such roles could include people with Asperger's Syndrome. Is it ethically acceptable to target recruitment efforts at people with Asperger's Syndrome, in order to achieve peak productivity at Factory A?

SCENARIO 3:

Gene editing has become a reality. Is it ethically acceptable to edit the genes of an embryo to prevent a child from being born with physical or mental disabilities?

If we can't see that some of these scenarios are ethically problematic, then Fukuyama was correct when he wrote (2002:9): "Sorry, Your soul just died."

Description related to motivation

Some businesses will probably counteract the increasing global competition by increasing the outsourcing of parts of the business. However, this strategy will negatively affect all the workers who lose their jobs in the process. This will occur during the period when new technology, such as AI and robotics, is still being introduced in working life. In this transitional period, such a counter-reaction to competitive pressure will probably continue. In such a situation, people with disabilities will experience difficulties in the labour market. However, this section will mainly focus on the future scenario when new AI and robotics technology has been fully integrated into working life, and not on the transitional situation that exists at the moment. In other words, we will investigate the work opportunities and conditions for people with disabilities when this technology is fully integrated into the economy.

We do not overlook the fact that cost savings in low-cost countries will be a strategy that will also be operative in the Fourth Industrial Revolution. The main focus of this chapter, however, is related to how new technology can open up opportunities for people with disabilities.

Though, in the global competition, it is not only labour costs that will be focused on, but also the ability to innovate (Austin, 2019). In such a context, people with disabilities, especially those who are creative, will have an advantage, because creativity is a prerequisite for innovation.

Another competitive factor is related to quality. In high-precision industries, some people with disabilities, such as those with Asperger's Syndrome, may be preferable, because of their ability to go into depth and focus on the small details (Attwood, 2015). In many production processes, computer-based simulation programs will also be used. There are many people with disabilities who can perform maintenance and service on these simulation programs just as well as people without disabilities. Therefore, the new technology can help to motivate managers to employ people with disabilities in businesses with high-precision production.

In other words, in the Fourth Industrial Revolution, there will be at least three areas of the economy, where people with disabilities may be preferred in working life. These are areas where costs are under pressure, and where the new technology can solve this problem better than outsourcing. The second area is where you need innovation to be able to compete. Creative people will be in demand here. The third area is where there is a need to continuously improve quality in, e.g., high-precision industries. We have combined these three social mechanisms for what will motivate businesses to hire people with disabilities as shown in Figure 5.2.

Analysis related to motivation

Micro-signals can trigger macro behaviour. The simplest example is traffic lights at a crossroads (Schelling, 2006: 4). If the government authorities signal that

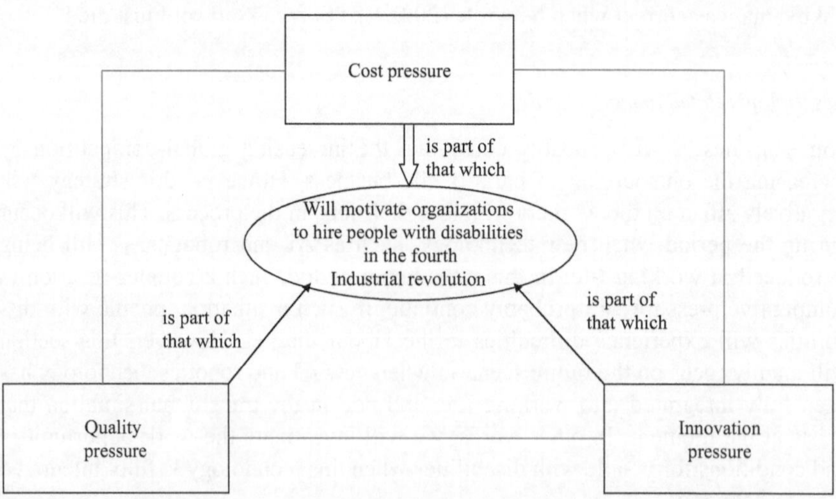

Figure 5.2 A framework for what will motivate organizations to employ people with disabilities in the Fourth Industrial Revolution (FIR).

employing people with disabilities will trigger resources from the public sector, then it seems reasonable to assume that this will trigger a type of behaviour that will result in people with disabilities being able to find work. One should not ignore the strength of such micro-signals, because they can trigger a type of macro behaviour that benefits all parties. Thomas Schelling (2006: 4) describes a scenario, "the misplaced mattress," regarding the relationship between micro motivation and macro behaviour. The traffic on a busy road is crawling along at a snail's pace. The problem is a misplaced mattress lying in the middle of the road which all the cars have to squeeze past. None of the drivers has any incentive to remove the mattress to help the other drivers behind them because this would be an extra inconvenience. The point is of course the motivation on which the individual has to act, or not act, and remove the mattress. If we transfer this analogy to people with disabilities looking for work, then the government authorities can motivate businesses to "remove any mattresses" so that "the queue flows freely."

We have shown above that in the Fourth Industrial Revolution, employing people with disabilities will, in many cases, be profitable for businesses, and not an act of charity. However, there is still "a mattress in the road," because people still have attitudes that belong to another era; i.e., the view that giving people with disabilities employment is an act of charity. Old attitudes can be changed by giving businesses incentives to hire people with disabilities. The rationale is that new practices would show that these people are just as important to the achievement of a business's goal as any other person. The incentives can be in the form of new legislation or material rewards. The idea is that micro motives change macro behaviour, which was Schelling's (2006) point. Removing "the mattress from the middle of the road" in the example above could easily have been done analogously by introducing a law that said that those who removed objects from the road, which obstructed or were a danger to traffic, and could document this, would receive a reward representing roughly 10 per cent of a monthly salary. This would result in the quick removal of many "mattresses" in social systems that result in queue formation.

Theoretical points related to motivation

Most people are motivated by a purpose. They have preferences, they seek to achieve goals, they want to minimize the use of resources to achieve the goal, and so on. What motivates us may be different from what motivates others, but we all seek to achieve something with our behaviour and actions. When we consider what will be appropriate to do, we always reflect on what others will do in relation to our behaviour and actions. This is one of the reasons why we don't stand up at a football match to see better, because if others stand up in front of us, then we will end up seeing less than if we had remained sitting. As a general rule, other people's behaviour is therefore always taken into account when we are deciding what to do. We thus have a situation where our behaviour is conditioned by what others want to do. Metaphorically speaking, we have a mattress in the road in front of us, and need incentives to get it removed.

Proposition: We often decide how to act based on how we think those around us will act.

People adapt to their environment. When the environmental conditions change, people have to adapt to them. This is one of the principles of the theory of evolution. On the other hand, many people do not just adapt, but modify the environment to best suit their needs, which others will then need to adapt to. Large organizations can create their own business environment, and thus their own and others' futures. In other words, it is not only the principles of evolutionary theory that are important regarding adapting and succeeding, but also creative and innovative processes, i.e., creating one's own future, by creating the environment to which you and others need to adapt to.

Individual incentives, perceptions, and preferences create a collective behaviour that we as individuals are not aware of, and in some contexts do not want either. It is in such contexts that micro motives can lead to macro behaviour. This can be related to the above analogy of Schelling's mattress. Through our individual perceptions, which do not need to be based on facts, we create a collective behaviour through network mechanisms. By removing this "mattress" we can create a future that suits everyone, including those with disabilities.

Proposition: Changing our own reaction to other people's behaviour will create a different future.

Practical utility related to motivation

The more people are excluded from working life because they have disabilities, the greater will be their dependency on welfare, and consequently an increase in costs and in taxation for working people. By providing jobs for those people with disabilities, the greater the likelihood that working people will fare better financially, and those with disabilities will also improve their incomes and well-being.

The disabled have lower income and poorer housing than other people. In other words, to avoid having a segregated society based on disability, one solution would be to change attitudes and behaviour by giving businesses incentives to hire disabled workers. Another solution would be to change the laws that exclude the disabled from the labour market. For example, a type of affirmative action that ensures equal employment opportunities for the disabled, by giving disabled job applicants preferential rights in relation to the competition with other applicants.

The organizing principle behind hiring new employees is often governed by habits, ideas, and tradition. If enough people involved in the hiring process have a generalized opinion about people with disabilities, this can infect others in the hiring process and lead to a biased collective behaviour. In other words, people often generalize and discriminate on the basis of a single case, without checking the factual basis for what the person with disability can bring to the organization.

We need to deal with the discriminatory social mechanisms, in order to change our reaction to the perceptions or behaviour of others. If we do not address these social mechanisms, and do not change our own reactions to the behaviour of others, then we will only reinforce collective discrimination. What are the social mechanisms that result in the discrimination against people with disabilities in working life?

We have selected five such social mechanisms:

1. **Incentives motivate behaviour**: If organizations are motivated through incentives to hire people with disabilities, then their behaviour changes.
2. **Rulings through legislation motivate behaviour**: If a law is passed giving people with disabilities preferential rights in relation to hiring processes, then organizations will change their behaviour.
3. **Integration affects perception**: The more we get used to working with people with disabilities, the more we will change our perception and then our behaviour.
4. **Individual behaviour creates collective patterns**: The dynamics of understanding collective patterns are difficult to spot. These dynamics are not transparent, and it therefore often creates perceptions that do not match the realities. The point is that perceptions become realities that we are then governed by.
5. **Patterns and structures affect our perceived freedom**: The patterns that have been established through myths, stories, and tradition help to maintain structures that do not always benefit people.

Sub-conclusion related to motivation

In this section, we examine the following question: How can organizations be motivated to hire people with disabilities? The short answer is various types of incentives and mandates by law.

It is perhaps rather naive and over-optimistic to believe that organizations will change their policies regarding the well-being and inclusion of people with disabilities on the basis of the well-presented arguments of others. We are of the opinion that organizations are motivated by three factors. Firstly, it needs to be profitable for businesses to employ people with disabilities. For example, in some cases people with disabilities will be able to carry out work better than others. Secondly, businesses can employ people with disabilities if the government provides subsidies, so that businesses do not suffer financially. Thirdly, the government can introduce mandates by law.

Attitudes

In this section we examine the following question: How can different attitudes affect the employment of people with disabilities?

Attitudes can be the result of the models we use when we plan social development. If the main model is based on the idea that economic growth is the only factor that matters regarding people's quality of life, then this provides guidelines for both attitudes and actions. In such models, which are used by the World Bank and the International Monetary Fund (IMF), amongst others, economic growth is viewed as being the most important indicator of prosperity. In this context, economic inequality,

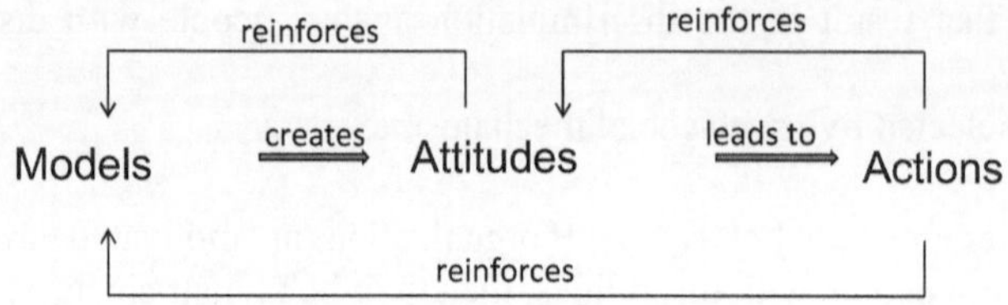

Figure 5.3 A cybernetic model for the "capabilities approach."

and how we treat people with disabilities, is viewed in relation to how this promotes or inhibits economic growth. It is in such a context that one can say that models of society become models for how we develop society. If economic growth is assumed to be the most important indicator of the quality of life and well-being, then people with disabilities will come second. If, on the other hand, we start from what people are able to do and to be, a "capabilities approach" (Austin, 2019; Gangas, 2019; Dalziel & Sunders, 2019), then this creates completely different attitudes and actions towards people with disabilities. We have shown this relationship in Figure 5.3.

Questions that are relevant in the capabilities approach in relation to people with disabilities and the development of models for this category in working life, are as follows:

1. What are they capable of doing?
2. What are the real possibilities?
3. What limitations are there?
4. How is the situation in the various countries in relation to people with disabilities?
5. Which policy is best suited to increase the well-being and satisfaction of people with disabilities?

Narratives related to attitudes

Case letter 1: Robots and attitudes

As robots become an integral part of social development and a regular part of working life, interaction between humans and robots will be focused on. The attitude towards intelligent robots, and their role in the work team, will be put to the test. Some research shows that if you carry out team-building activities with humans and robots, the attitude towards the robots will change positively after such activities (Carlson et al, 2015). Furthermore, the same research found that attitudes changed even more in a positive direction when the tasks were solved satisfactorily (Carlson et al., 2015: 113–123). If we connect this research to design for inclusion in working life, then it seems reasonable to say that in heterogeneous groups, where people with disabilities participate, people will develop positive attitudes towards each other after such team-building activities, where robots are also part of the team-building project.

Case letter 2: Skin deep

A person's disability represents a tiny part of their overall capacity as a human, just like the colour of their skin occurs in a thin layer of epidermis. Even so, attitudes to that paper-thin layer of coloured skin and to people's disabilities can be extremely stigmatizing and often lead to social exclusion. In nature, diversity is a powerful survival mechanism. Why shouldn't the same be true of diversity in social systems? Diversity in social systems can be perceived as threatening, while in nature it is a mechanism that helps ensure survival. Is it possible that our attitudes are playing games with us and as a result could diminish the resilience of our society? On the one hand, diversity is perceived as a threat. On the other hand, society cannot survive without diversity. As case letter 1 implied, collaboration, connection, and co-creation can be easy ways to change attitudes to diversity. As we co-create, we gradually tear down the barriers that our attitudes have built between us. By engaging in co-creative activities, we can find that there is so much more to a person than their disability, rather than allowing ourselves to get hung up on a minor disability or a paper-thin layer of skin colour.

Description related to attitudes

If collaboration and co-creation are the solution to many of the challenges people with disabilities face in working life, why is this not used to a greater extent to change people's attitudes? Today, we can connect to the rest of the population with a keystroke on our computers, so connectivity is not the problem, because then we would have already gotten rid of the challenges of employing people with disabilities in organizations. Could the real problem in organizations be the fear of diversity? From such a perspective, it is not the people who have some disability that represent a problem in social systems, but the people who fear diversity, because they inhibit the system's chances of survival. Understood from such a perspective, it is a great irony that people still talk about problems related to people with disabilities. If diversity stimulates creativity and innovation, and these are the main social mechanisms if organizations are to succeed in the Fourth Industrial Revolution, then it is the people who fear diversity who pose the largest problem for the progress of organizations, institutions, and other social systems.

When we are faced with challenges in our own organization, we tend to become spectators. As spectators, we become passive observers of people with disabilities being disregarded in hiring processes (Sarpong, 2019). We tend to focus on the small differences that divide us than what unites us. By changing our perspective, not only will our attitudes change, but also our actions.

Attitudes can be changed by actions. Just think of Dr Martin Luther King's "I have a dream" speech that was delivered on 28 August 1963. This speech changed attitudes towards African Americans. Admittedly it took time, but slowly and surely a lot has changed after this speech. One could wish someone would give a similar speech focusing on the needs of people with disabilities in working life. In other words, the models we use to understand and explain social phenomena create attitudes, which then trigger actions.

Analysis related to attitudes

As we move into the Fourth Industrial Revolution, the reason for writing a book about people with disabilities is that we need to take seriously their struggle to live a dignified life. We know that with the new technology this will be possible for everyone, because automation increases productivity and frees up resources, so that everyone will be able to benefit from what they are good at. This should not be understood to mean that everyone with a disability needs help to perform their work tasks satisfactorily. On the contrary, there are many people with disabilities who perform excellent work, and there are even more who could do so if they were given the opportunity. For those people with disabilities who want to enter the labour market, it is often a question of attitude. On the other hand, some people with disabilities need special accommodations in the workplace in order to do their job satisfactorily. New automation processes and increased productivity will present more opportunities for people with disabilities to enter working life. This may sound like a paradox, but it is precisely in this paradox that the solution lies. The technology will make it possible to use people who need other resources, in order to carry out their work tasks. In contrast, the core of the paradox lies in the social system of which this technology is a part. It's not complicated, it's not difficult, and it's not even a technological problem. The problem is related to the simple question: Do we wish to help people with disabilities so that they are included in working life? If the answer is "no," then the problem will be left for society and those with disabilities to deal with. If the answer is "yes," then it is only a practical question of how we should approach the problem. It all boils down to whether we really want to do something for people who have disabilities.

Economists and politicians focus on the growth of production and prosperity, while most people focus on having a meaningful and dignified life. This applies to everyone, both those with disabilities and those who do not need special accommodations in working life. However, there need not be a contradiction between economic growth and a dignified life for people. It is largely the attitude we have towards people that determines the models we apply to organizations and social systems. If instead of focusing only on economic growth, we instead focus on people's quality of life, then the productivity increases, that the new technology will necessarily lead to, can be used to increase the quality of life for many people.

Theoretical points related to attitudes

Why are people with a disability often excluded from working life? This question implies a whole ideological framework of explanations. We have written above that in relation to attitudes, it is the models we use to understand and explain society that are decisive for how we answer this question. Therefore, from this perspective, it is the models that are the intervention point for understanding people's attitudes. A conceptualization of these models is often hidden from most people, including those who use the models. Therefore, we refer here to these models as "hidden models." It is these hidden models that in turn create our attitudes towards integration versus exclusion of people with disabilities in working life.

The hidden models can be made explicit by the following division[8]:

- Economic.
- Political.
- Cultural.
- Relational.

The economic models can be divided into two main types, efficiency models and well-being models. The political models can be divided into capitalist models and "solidarity" models. The cultural models can be divided into tradition-bound models and "family" models. The relational models can be divided into social inclusion and social exclusion.

We have illustrated this division of the hidden models, in order to make them explicit.

Figure 5.4 shows that there are eight different sub-models, which can then be combined in n(n-1) ways, i.e., 56 different combinations, if we imagine that the sub-models can also have different relationships to each other. However, the point here is not to provide a mathematical explanation, but to show that "hidden" models can be made explicit by reflection. The purpose of making the hidden models explicit is to gain an understanding of the different attitudes that influence the hiring processes of people with disabilities.

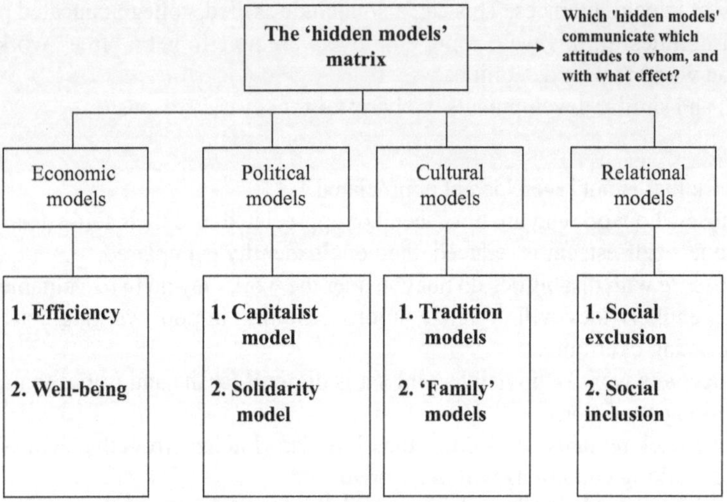

Figure 5.4 Making the "hidden models" explicit.

Practical utility related to attitudes

"Hidden" models have concrete consequences for people with disabilities. On the one hand, the models can lead to people with disabilities being "hidden away." On the other hand, the hidden models can lead to social inclusion. If we fail to make the models explicit, then we will not know which models form the basis for attitudes. If we do not know how attitudes are formed, it will also be difficult to introduce measures to change attitudes. Many people with disabilities work on contracts outside the regulated labour market. In this way, they are "kept hidden" and become part of an invisible workforce. This can be compared to women's unpaid housework during the post-war period which was not included in GDP calculations – in other words, it was "hidden" labour. Many people with disabilities become a cost item on the national expenditure on disability. Instead of contributing to national expenditure it would be more expedient if they were able to work, given some extra resources. In other words, this would benefit society and contribute to the self-esteem of the disabled persons who were thus able to work.

There are many types of "hidden" work that people with disabilities do, in order to earn extra income. For example, computer sales, crowdsourcing, call-centre employees, virtual receptionists, virtual information providers, association ambassadors on the web, service engineers on the web, etc. In other words, there are many areas of work that people with disabilities can be involved in. The point in our context is that many of these work functions are "hidden" with no employment contracts, or inadequate contracts. By making this type of work invisible, working conditions are being obscured; this can result in a situation where disabled workers are carrying out work without a legally binding contract. Examples of this type of work and contracts are the so-called unpaid internships. If such unpaid internships are made into a system, this can result in a situation where employers never actually "hire" workers, but are nevertheless able to build a workforce consisting entirely of unpaid internees. This can also include skilled, college-educated people with disabilities. In this way, some employers are able to get a "free" workforce based on workers with disabilities.

This and similar developments are harmful for several reasons:

1. Work that is not "seen" is not appreciated.
2. Those who work and are not "seen" or appreciated lose their self-esteem.
3. If one's self-esteem is reduced, then one's identity is impaired.
4. If people with disabilities do not consider the work they do to be valuable, then it is unlikely they will organize unions, resulting in poor working conditions persisting over time.
5. If people's work is "invisible," then it is difficult for the authorities to monitor working conditions.
6. If the work remains "invisible," then it is also "hidden" from the legal system, and working conditions will deteriorate.
7. "Invisible" work and thus also the "invisible" workforce remain in the unregulated labour market.

Sub-conclusion related to attitudes

In this section we have examined the following question: How can different attitudes affect the employment of people with disabilities? The short answer is that the "hidden" models create diverse attitudes towards people with disabilities in working life (cf. Figure 5.4). The slightly longer answer is that by examining what constitutes the attitudes towards people with disabilities, one can deal with attitudes regarding the "invisible" work that is performed in the economy. The invisible work in this context is all work that in one way or another creates economic value for society, paid and unpaid, but which is overlooked, made virtual, pushed out of sight for customers and others, devalued by employers, employees, and outside the control of the authorities. Some of the invisible work that is carried out by people with disabilities is paid work, whereas, other work is poorly paid or not paid for at all. It is only by making the invisible work visible that the working conditions can be improved.

Leadership

In this section, we will examine the following question: How can different types of leadership influence the employment of people with disabilities?

Leaders do not need to believe that it is only for humanitarian reasons that people with disabilities should be hired. In the innovation economy, where creativity and innovation are the most important social mechanisms for success, research shows that businesses that have a large degree of diversity among their employees are also the businesses that succeed better than those that do not have such diversity (Sweeney & Bothwick, 2016). Businesses that hire talented people are better positioned to outperform their competitors. In this context, people with disabilities are an untapped source of talent. This is a crucial lesson that leaders need to learn. Diversity, no matter how you define it, will, without exception, promote creativity in an organization. Organizations are essentially organized around their production, products, and delivery of services (Beer, 1985). However, the world around us is changing rapidly, especially during a time of rapid technological developments (Johannessen, 2018; 2018a). Therefore, organizations need to change their original structure to adapt to the new technologies of AI and robotics. As we move towards the Fourth Industrial Revolution, this is becoming the most important task facing leaders.

Narratives related to leadership

Case letter 1: Can robots object to the decisions of senior executives?

Imagine a future in which robotics and AI have become integral to the operations of most businesses and play a decisive role in collecting and analysing data and implementing decisions. In addition, suppose that the expectations and preferences of different groups within the organization are identified and supplied as feedback to the relevant information systems. The organization's leadership philosophy emphasizes diversity and the organization has a workplace inclusion policy to facilitate the employment of people with disabilities. In such a situation, we can imagine an organization's information processing system being globally connected with the systems of other organizations in the same sector. In other words, these companies would have "intelligent information processing systems." Imagine such systems being instructed by a particular leader to conduct certain operations. The question we put to our readers is as follows: Should a robot/information processing system be designed so that it can object and refuse to carry out orders from senior managers if the robot/system has calculated that these orders conflict with one or more of the following considerations?

a. Financial expectations.
b. Ethical expectations.
c. The requirements of people with disabilities and expectations regarding their performance.
d. Other issues.

Description related to leadership

Diversity, disability, and social inclusion have traditionally been left to the HR department, and sometimes linked to corporate social responsibility (CSR). This is a model that largely derives from classical industrial thinking, where taking care of people with disabilities was viewed as a social responsibility. AI and robotics will be increasingly important in most industries in the Fourth Industrial Revolution, which will increase automation, performance and efficiency, and generate new jobs. Against this background, diversity, creativity and innovation will be especially important (Anielski, 2018). In such a context, creating employment opportunities for people with disabilities will be a strategy for promoting creative and innovative processes in organizations, rather than a social responsibility.

Thus, traditionally, organizational leaders have targeted recruitment and hiring of people with disabilities as part of corporate social responsibility. However, in the Fourth Industrial Revolution hiring people with disabilities will be good for businesses, because this will most probably contribute to stimulating creativity and innovation processes. This can be explained by the fact that there will be a demand for different kinds of competences. In other words, the focus will be on creativity and innovation rather than just efficiency. Of course, efficiency and productivity will still be important, but the increased use of AI and robotics will stimulate automation processes, resulting in more efficient production. Consequently, there will be an increased demand for people who can contribute to creative and innovation processes.

On the one hand, organizational leaders are obliged to follow the law regarding the rights of disabled people. On the other hand, management also needs to pay attention to efficiency and productivity. In this pressured situation, the capabilities of disabled workers are often undermined, and they are often not hired. We have seen examples where leaders reject well-qualified people simply because they have lost an arm or a leg in war or in traffic accidents (Hunt, 1966). Such discriminatory practices led to the development of a social model for disability, where it is how society is organized that is disabling, not a person's disability (Oliver, 2012). A leaders' "hidden" models can have an impact on both their attitudes and actions. Disability can be categorized into three models: the individual model, the social model, and the medical model. The individual model, also called "the tragedy model," focuses on the problems faced by the disabled person resulting from their impairments, and thus also the help they need. The social model has been referred to above. The medical model of disability refers to the disability that is the result of a physical or mental condition, and which may lead to a reduction in the individual's capacity to function in various situations. In this section, we will focus on a systemic framework, which integrates the three models. Figure 5.5 shows the systemic framework of the three models.

Analysis related to leadership

Social inclusion is not a social responsibility for businesses. In order to gain access to the best talents in an age where AI and robotics will automate most repetitive work functions, it is irrelevant whether a talented person has a mental disability, such as Asperger's Syndrome, or a physical disability requiring the use of a wheelchair. The most important factor in an employment situation is that the individual is able to carry out his/her work efficiently, not that he/she is not like everyone else in all respects. In the Fourth Industrial Revolution, the best talents from around the globe will form part of a competence pool that businesses and individuals will be able to access. This is already happening today. For example, if you call a Norwegian helpline number for Booking.com in order to book an apartment, such as "Sir Gamle Skole" in Denmark, you may very well be connected to a

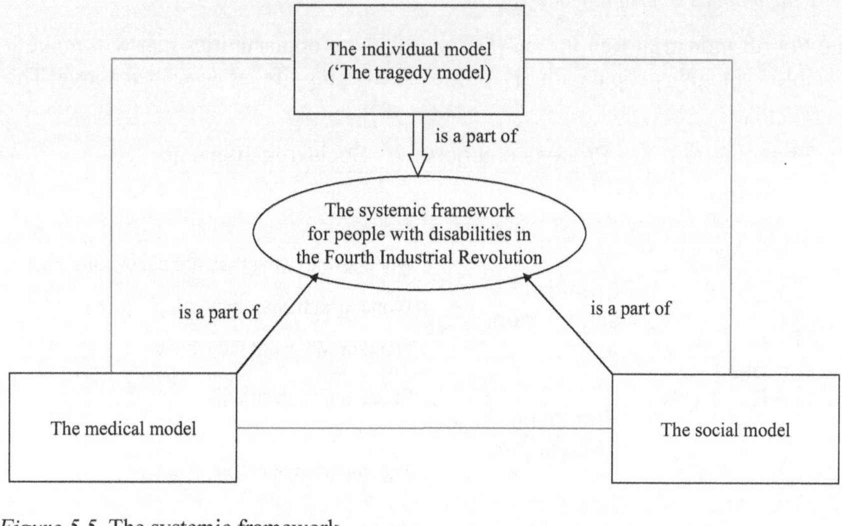

Figure 5.5 The systemic framework.

Norwegian-speaking person located somewhere on the Malaga coast in Spain. This person may probably be a contract worker; whether or not this person is disabled will be completely irrelevant for your needs as a customer, as long as the person in question can supply you with the information you need. In other words, the continual development of new technology in the Fourth Industrial Revolution will result in many more such work scenarios in the future.

Diversity is not only linked to gender, age, educational background, and ethnicity. Diversity is also linked to social inclusion of people with disabilities. Why is diversity important in the Fourth Industrial Revolution (FIR)? We know that the drivers for success in FIR will be creativity and innovation (Johannessen, 2018). We also know that creativity is best promoted where diversity prevails (Johannessen, 2018a). This is the economic rationale for inclusion and diversity.

A leader's job in relation to inclusion and diversity is, among other things, to make people feel protected and accepted in the workplace, even if they have some special needs that others do not have. When people feel unique and special in a positive sense, they will perform at their best. In this context, there are two factors that define good leaders. This is to create a work situation where employees feel involved in the work processes that lead the organization towards its goal. To create commitment, three social mechanisms can be decisive. This is to allow the individual, regardless of their special needs, to work with what he/she is passionate about. In addition, the person should be guided in the direction of what he/she is good at and which he/she masters. In order to create an optimal work situation, two social mechanisms are crucial. These are involvement and making sure that employees feel they are being "seen," i.e., that their commitment and work are acknowledged.

We have developed a model for managerial success in the Fourth Industrial Revolution (FIR) (Figure 5.6).

Theoretical points related to leadership

The Fourth Industrial Revolution (FIR) will create opportunities that will make it possible to include people with disabilities in working life, as described above. The

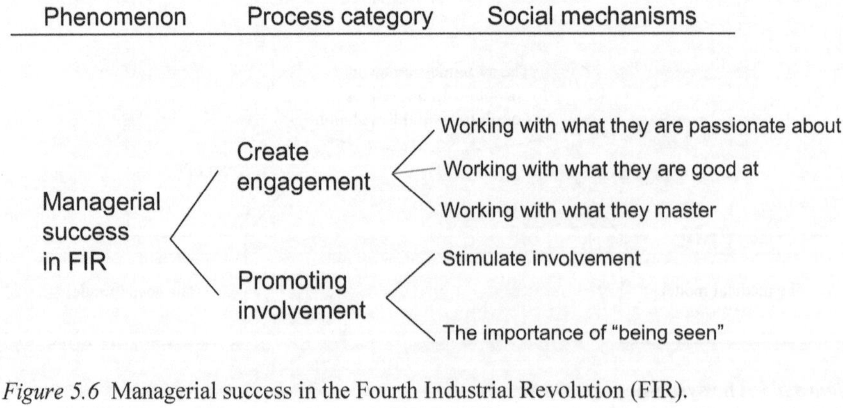

Figure 5.6 Managerial success in the Fourth Industrial Revolution (FIR).

question remains, however, whether this will occur or not, and what it will take to make this happen. What we do know is that if employees feel disconnected from their organization they will not be able to perform to the best of their ability, so that the organization is able to achieve its goals. Of course, this does not only apply to people with disabilities, but to everyone in an organization. It is the feeling of being socially integrated that triggers creative energy. However, this does not necessarily require that employees are physically present at the workplace. You can still be socially integrated, even if you live in Spain, but work for a company in England. Physical presence at the workplace is something that belongs to a past industrial logic. Today, employees can be socially included in a virtual business environment that is continuously constituted by various projects in the global economy.

Employees need to see that everyone can achieve success, regardless of the special needs the employees may have, because employees can find themselves in a changed situation, where they need special arrangements, in order to carry out their work.

What leaders do, and what they don't do, is seen and commented on by employees. The biggest group coming up into the workforce today is the millennial generation[9] (also called Generation Y) who expect leaders to make sure that their work tasks make sense to them, that they can work autonomously without any unnecessary control, and that their work is linked to a purpose.[10] This also applies to people with disabilities. They are not like the generation before them, who had to stand with cap in hand, in order to get work. The millennial generation expects the leader to see them as a whole person, and not only in relation to any special accommodation they may need.

Jokes and stories, which are only intended as fun, are often in their consequences a type of micro-aggression (Sue, 2016). Such behaviour can result in undesirable attitudes in workplaces. These jokes and stories may be about sexual orientation, ethnicity, class, gender, age, language dialects, people with disabilities, religious affiliation, and so on. Sue (2016: 574) defines micro-aggression as follows: "brief and commonplace daily verbal, behavioral, or environmental indignities, whether intentional or unintentional, that communicate hostile, derogatory, or negative racial slights and insults toward people."

Proposition: If the leader manages to engage employees, and create the feeling of involvement, then everyone will feel connected and included, which will promote managerial success.

Practical utility related to leadership

Leadership should always be able to foster a culture of employee engagement to some degree. In order to attract the best talent, the organization's reputation in the market is important. If it is the case that Generation Y, more than other generations, seek purpose in their work, and in addition, that they want to work autonomously and not feel controlled, then it is important that organizations manage to project a reputation that reflects this type of work environment. Against this background, leaders need to be actively engaged in recruitment policy. If you are looking for the best talents, it is not enough to post a traditional advertisement for a vacant position. New employees need to be integrated into the company culture, so the company culture remains healthy and does not take an undesirable direction. Of course, it is not the case that all people are equally talented. It is the leader's task to identify the employees who perform above average, and who also help colleagues to perform better. It is the talented employees who manage to develop a creative field who are important for businesses. It is therefore crucial that the leader rewards these employees in one way or another. The leader needs to ensure that these employees are rewarded to an extent that is commensurate with what competitors may be willing to give. It is precisely these employees who function as a social mechanism for creating commitment and participation among the other employees. It is never the case that everyone is equally committed and involved in an organization.

It is often the case that diversity and inclusion coupled with talented employees develops a creative energy field in an organization. This creative energy field tends to spread throughout the organization if nurtured properly (Gratton, 2007). For the leader, it is one of the most important tasks at the entrance to the Fourth Industrial Revolution, to develop as many such creative fields of energy as possible. If the leader fails to develop creative energy fields, then an organizational death spiral may occur. In such a situation, employees mainly focus on their own interests, and any ideas they may have they keep to themselves. On the other hand, employees may be committed, but show little participation. In such a situation, those who are committed will have no motive to encourage others to participate in activities that create organizational success. The individual with talent will tend to think: "What's in it for me?" One can also imagine that the commitment is low, but that employees actively participate in the work of the organization. This is an organizational culture where employees feel that it is necessary to participate, in order to keep their jobs without being actively engaged in the work. Such behaviour will not trigger creative fields, but will be able to maintain high productivity in organizations where "business as usual" is the most important thing.

In the Fourth Industrial Revolution, there are few organizations that will survive with such an attitude amongst employees.

We have developed a typology for the leader's two most important functions at the entrance to the Fourth Industrial Revolution (Figure 5.7).

Sub-conclusion related to leadership

In this section, we examine the following question: How can different types of leadership influence the employment of people with disabilities?

The short answer is that the leaders who can create a large degree of commitment and a large degree of participation amongst employees will be the most successful leaders at the entrance to the Fourth Industrial Revolution. This also applies to employees with disabilities. To increase commitment, leaders have three social mechanisms they can use: The employees should be allowed to work with what they are passionate about. They should be allowed to work with what they are good at, and they need to master what they do. To promote participation, there are two

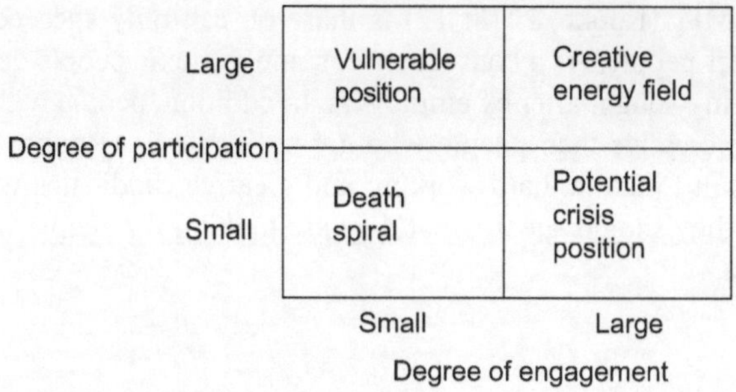

Figure 5.7 Degrees of commitment and participation at the entrance to the Fourth Industrial Revolution.

social mechanisms a leader can use: Employees should feel that they are involved in the processes that concern them, and that their work is acknowledged and they are "seen."

The working environment

In this section, we examine the following question: How can different attitudes affect the employment of people with disabilities?

Feeling like an outsider at work can result in emotional distress. If efficiency and productivity are what we only measure success by, then many of the values that govern our lives will become secondary. In such a working environment, people with disabilities will need to have capabilities above average, because they are often viewed as an extra cost by companies. If money is the measure of all things, then a worker's identity will be created and maintained by the social mechanisms that create the income in an organization, e.g., efficiency and productivity. In such a working environment, people with disabilities will only be able to create their identity by being better than the others. Such a working environment will always have a threshold, where emotional distress can become too great for workers with disabilities.

Narratives related to the workplace

Case letter 1: Dyslexia is my superpower

Feeble-minded, debilitated, imbecilic, idiotic. These words were applied to some people with disabilities in the 1970s. Words have an impact on both those who utter them and those they refer to. When Margaret Rooke (2018) gave her book the title *Dyslexia is my SUPERPOWER (most of the time)*, it was clear that she had understood that the way in which one frames a situation determines how that situation will be understood, both by the person doing the framing and by others, such as colleagues in a workplace. The best thing about dyslexia, writes Catherine Drennan, a professor at MIT (Rooke, 2018: 12) is that you can only succeed by working harder than other people. As a consequence, some dyslexic people develop a work ethic that is highly sought after by employers. In addition, people with dyslexia are generally more creative than people who are not dyslexic (Rooke, 2016). If HR departments want to attract hard-working and creative candidates when advertising vacancies, they should specify that they are looking for people with a specific talent: Dyslexia.

Description related to leadership

People with disabilities learn over time to deal with their problems by thinking "outside the box," i.e., by exploring ideas that are creative and that are not limited by guidelines or custom. A leader can create a work environment that includes people with disabilities quite simply by listening to their needs and fulfilling their wishes. This is not done for humanist reasons, but for reasons of capital logic. What is meant by this? People with disabilities, such as dyslexia in the above narrative, are often hard-working, creative, and determined. This is not unlike the character traits Angela Duckworth (2017) found in her research regarding creative and successful people. These people also had a burning desire to succeed. They were persistent and never gave up. This is not unlike the findings Margaret Rooke (2018) found regarding people diagnosed with dyslexia.

Leaders often believe that workplace accommodations for employees with disabilities are typically costly. Therefore, employing people with disabilities is often done out of a desire to show social responsibility, be humanistic, and show human consideration. Moreover, companies are required by law to reserve a small percentage of their jobs for disabled people.

Effective and above-average leaders will have different ideas about hiring people with disabilities. They know that many people with disabilities have a type of GRIT[11] that Angela Duckworth (2017) found in her research, and which Margaret Rooke (2018) also emphasizes in her research. The leaders with greater insight will hire people with disabilities to build a positive working environment consisting of hard-working people, who are also creative. This will provide a foundation for developing creative energy fields in an organization, which will foster innovation and increase productivity (Gratton, 2007).

Leaders and HR departments need to have insight about what people with disabilities can contribute to an organization. This is largely where the challenge lies, i.e., leaders and HR departments often have a lack of insight regarding this. It might be said that these leaders and departments work according to an industrial logic where production needs to be flawless. However, it is precisely this type of thinking that can result in mediocrity, because in the global innovation economy, and especially at the entrance to the Fourth Industrial Revolution, it is precisely commitment, persistence, moral courage, and a burning desire to make a difference that will lead the way from mediocrity to success (Duckworth, 2017; Johannessen, 2020; Johannessen et al., 2020).

Analysis related to leadership

If we imagine a working environment where the well-being of the employees is central, then we will have the prerequisite for developing an organization where people's welfare and satisfaction (Seligman, 2011) are given priority before profit. In such a working environment, having disabilities will be a strength and not a weakness (Rooke, 2018). If, on the other hand, we adopt a profit logic that guides development in an organization, then the well-being of the employees will be viewed in relation to productivity. In other words, if the working environment is good, then this will increase productivity and income. Using such a logic, the well-being of employees will become a means to achieve another goal, namely productivity and income. The logic of profit leads to greater economic inequality. The growing economic inequality has many negative consequences for people and the environment (Piketty, 2015). By focusing on people's well-being, satisfaction, commitment, and feeling of meaning with what they do, it will be possible to create an inclusive working environment, where there is an awareness that people are different and bring different things to an organization (Seligman, 2011; 2017).

Businesses that promote the implementation of disability inclusion policies, and also focus on the well-being of workers, will foster a working environment where workers can develop their full potential. Such a working environment will ensure job satisfaction and well-being. This will be in accordance with Maslow's (2013) hierarchy of needs, where well-being, belonging, esteem, and self-actualization are at the upper top half of the hierarchy.

In order to achieve an organizational logic, which promotes well-being, purpose, and satisfaction (Seligman, 2011) will require that the profit logic is restructured so that people's needs have priority and profit comes second. The paradox is that if you put people's needs before profit, the system's sustainability will be increased, and thus the system's earnings will also be secured over time (Korton, 2012; Anielski, 2018: 1–8).

What is the purpose of a business? If the answer to this question is to mainly maximize the shareholders' profits, then this may have a negative impact on the working environment. If, on the other hand, the answer is to also promote the well-being of employees and promote the sustainability of the environment, then we will be able to develop an inclusive working life.

Theoretical points related to leadership

AI and robotics will displace many jobs in the Fourth Industrial Revolution, due to workplace automation. The question is how this will affect those with disabilities. It is highly probable that the robots of the future will have superpowers, but they will not necessarily resemble humans. For example, virtual robotics will be located in virtual environments, and cloud robotics, or cloud computing, will be able to provide input for robotic devices. The robotics superpowers will be accessed by organizations when needed. For those with disabilities, this is probably good news, because where they previously had a disability, they may now have an advantage. This is shown by the example of Margaret Rooke (2018), where she points out that dyslexia can be a "superpower" in some contexts, or Greta Thunberg, who likens Asperger's Syndrome to a "superpower."[12] It may be imagined that the superpowers of the intelligent robots will give people with disabilities an advantage over others. With the increased development and use of intelligent robots they have an advantage, because they will be able to harness their creative powers, and use their burning desire to accomplish their goals.

It's safe to say that in the coming years robotics will transform workplaces, when work will be increasingly done by intelligent machines. Robotics will assist nurses, teachers, carpenters, plumbers, doctors, and so on. Robots will be all around us, and be able to see and hear us, and respond to our needs and wishes (Nourbakhsh, 2013: xiv). In other words, robotics and AI will radically change work and working environments as we move towards the Fourth Industrial Revolution.

Robotics research is largely about developing robots for control, sensory feedback, and information processing, and interaction with the environment based on sensors and actuators (Nourbakhsh, 2013: xiv). Further development of robotics will radically change working conditions and work relationships (Vallas & Kovalainen, 2019: 1):

1. Jobs for life are a thing of the past.
2. Permanent positions are a thing of the past.
3. Full-time employment is a thing of the past.

New developments indicate that people will be able to do their jobs where it best suits them; e.g., when they can deliver services digitally. For people with disabilities, this new development may very well be advantageous, because they can choose the time and place for working, and the amount of effort they wish to invest in their work.

Proposition: New technology, such as AI and robotics, can diminish or eliminate some of the barriers faced by people with disabilities in working life, and create new opportunities.

Practical utility related to leadership

Persons with disabilities are not a homogenous group – they have different capabilities and needs. The different types of needs place different demands on working environments. A rough division of the types of needs can be made according to physical needs for support and cognitive needs for support.

People with physical disabilities, such as wheelchair users, will need workplace accommodations. In many instances, this will require the removal of architectural barriers. This may require special architectural design.

If a person has little need for physical support, and little need of cognitive support, then the work environment will not need any special accommodation. For example, this may concern someone who has undergone hip surgery, someone who is blind in one eye after a stroke, or people with dyslexia.

People with cognitive disabilities may require a specially designed workplace. However, it is often the case that employers can receive funding to remunerate the cost of adapting the workplace for staff with cognitive disabilities. This can contribute to these disabled people being able to live a more worthwhile life.

People with considerable physical and cognitive disabilities will often be able to find work in sheltered workshops; these specially designed workplaces provide a controlled and safe work environment.

We have developed a typology for people with disabilities. The figure makes a distinction between workplaces that are dependent on government funding to finance the adaptation of the workplace, and those workplaces that do not receive funding (Figure 5.8).

Sub-conclusion related to leadership

In this section, we have examined the following question: How can different types of working environment affect the employment of people with disabilities?

The answer we have arrived at in this section can be summarized in the five points below:

1. A workplace that listens to the needs of employees.
2. A work environment that demands hard-working people.
3. A work environment that demands engagement.
4. A work environment that demands creativity.
5. A working environment that requires stamina.

Figure 5.9 shows a framework that answers the question in this section.

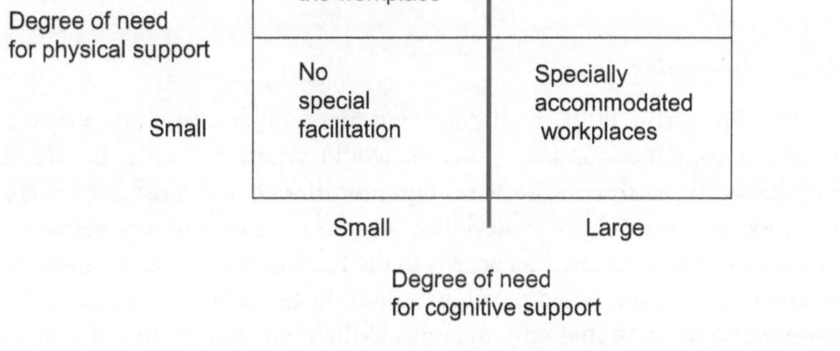

Figure 5.8 Typology for workplaces for people with disabilities.

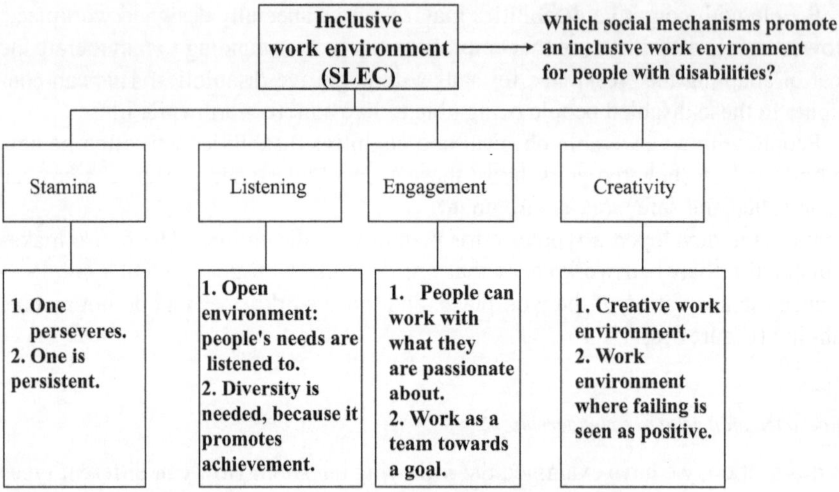

Figure 5.9 Inclusive working environment for people with disabilities.

Innovation and productivity

In this section, we examine the following question: How can innovation and productivity affect the employment of people with disabilities?

Implicit in this question is how the new technology in the Fourth Industrial Revolution, which will increase the informatization and automation of work processes, will affect the employment and working conditions of people with disabilities (Reese, 2018: 83). At the beginning of the 2000s, there emerged a digital divide between people (Warschauer, 2004: 1). However, with the further development of robotics and AI in the Fourth Industrial Revolution, this digital divide will become history. The further development of AI voice recognition software will allow people to interact with technology verbally. This will probably improve the lives and working conditions of many people with disabilities.

Narrative related to innovation and productivity

Case letter 1: Automation

In the 1990s and early 2000s, politicians and many others were concerned about how access to computers and the Internet would separate people, by creating a digital divide between those who were digitally literate and those who were not. To a large extent, this did not materialize, because the technology became more user-friendly and most people had access to the technology.[13] Today, many people are concerned that the increased development of AI and robotics will automate and rationalize workplaces so that only the most skilled will be able to keep their jobs. Some critics envision mass unemployment, with hordes of poor and unemployed people wandering restlessly around Europe, not unlike what happened at the fall of the Roman Empire. Of course, this will not happen. There will be neither mass unemployment nor wandering bands of poor men going from city to city in search of work. The reason is quite simple. No one, absolutely no one, will benefit from such a development. Although capitalism can be brutal, there is one thing that characterizes its basic mode: It is logical and rational. This is the main reason why mass unemployment will not develop, because capitalism is not served by hordes of poor people wandering the streets. The most likely scenario is that the new technology will lead to new jobs and new skills, which will also benefit people with disabilities. On the other hand, it would be expedient to start focusing more on the wage statistics rather than on the unemployment statistics, in order to gain an understanding of social developments at the entrance to the Fourth Industrial Revolution.

Description related to innovation and productivity

There may be new technology, but technological progress itself is nothing new. What is new however, is the increasing rate of change (Reese, 2018: 25–29). Of course, no one knows what will happen to workplaces in the future. However, we can examine the various assumptions and scenarios based on different knowledge perspectives and assessments.

The first scenario is that the new technology will fully eliminate entire categories of work, and supplant most workers. This scenario falls on its own unreasonableness, not because it is not possible, but because it is a scenario that no one wants. The political environment would wake up to a full-blooded nightmare if this were to become a reality. The capitalist system would wake up to a social revolution if this became a reality. Although it is technologically possible, it is not desired by anyone, absolutely no one.

The second scenario is that the new technology will automate most of the old work processes. This scenario, however, is completely different from the first scenario. The difference is that the new technology will create new work processes, demand new skills, and create new jobs. This will result in multiplier effects in the economy and social systems. Although many people will become redundant, many more new jobs will be created.

The third scenario is midway between the two previous scenarios. The new technology will remove some work functions and some people will be made redundant. However, new skills will also be in demand. Long-term unemployment will thus develop for some people. On the other hand, some of these people will be able to retrain, and gain the new skills that are in demand. Still others will be able to find various types of poorly paid service jobs; they may need to have several jobs to make ends meet (Johannessen, 2018; 2018a).

All three scenarios will result in a situation where it will be impossible to "robot-proof" jobs from automation. Everyone will be affected in one way or another by the new technology. Our point here, however, is that those with disabilities will be able to have a more meaningful working day with the further development of intelligent robots and artificial intelligence. This will especially apply when Singularity occurs (Kurtzweil, 2008; 2008; Johannessen, 2020).[14]

Regardless of whether intelligent robots and artificial intelligence take over all or some jobs from humans, this technological development will reinforce economic inequality. "The rich get richer and the poor get poorer" is not just a cliché, but has been shown to be the case through considerable research (Piketty, 2014; 2016). On the other hand, there is nothing to suggest that people with disabilities will not be able to develop competences that they can use, as knowledge workers or innovation workers, as shown in Figure 5.10.

Analysis related to innovation and productivity

People with disabilities are often characterized by the fact that their bodies and/or their cognitive capacities are different from what is considered "normal." We have discussed this above regarding dyslexia and Asperger's Syndrome, where Margaret Rooke points out that dyslexia can be a "superpower" (Rooke, 2016; 2018) in some contexts, and Greta Thunberg, who likens Asperger's Syndrome to a "superpower."[15] Can it be imagined that there are other diagnoses that can give people such a "superpower," when artificial intelligence and intelligent robots become part of everyday life in organizations? Possibly one can find something in the autism spectrum that can be an answer to part of the future competence that will be needed for accuracy and focus (Attwood, 2015).

People with disabilities are seeing new opportunities with the advances in technology, not least in relation to embodiment – that people's "reach" can extend into global areas using the Internet. In other words, the meaning of our bodies is being affected by the new technology, i.e., how our bodies sense the world and our orientation towards the world. This is a central theme that has been discussed by the philosopher Maurice Merleu-Ponty,[16] and the philosopher of technology, Don Ihde (2002), amongst others. The new technology has facilitated the use of home offices, which means that people no longer need to be located at a place of work. In other words, we can choose where 'home office' is located, for example at home or at our holiday cabin. One can venture the claim that the body has been "liberated" by

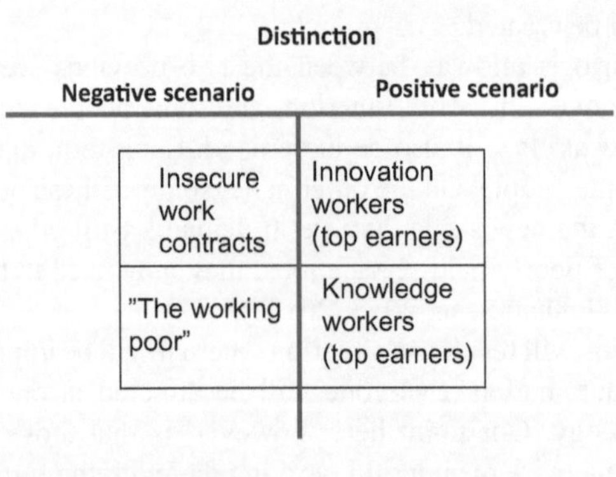

Figure 5.10 No jobs will be robot-proof.

the introduction of new technology, a tendency that will only increase as we move into the Fourth Industrial Revolution. This is possibly one of the biggest "bodily" revolutions in human history. People with disabilities no longer need to travel to a workplace, but can do their work where they choose – this is no less than a "revolution." The blind, the deaf, and people with physical challenges, can work in their familiar environment at home, and do not have to travel to a workplace every day. It may be argued that workplace relationships are important in working life. On the other hand, people also have relationships in their local environment. Deep relationships are almost absent in workplaces. In a very large survey, Gallup has found that people have approx. 0.8 deep relationships in the workplace (Dutton et al., 2003: 353–365). In other words, relationships of this type should therefore be no argument for having to do one's work at a specific workplace.

Theoretical points related to innovation and productivity

The Internet has expanded our perceptual range. The new technology has enabled us to "liberate" our bodies. Those who are possibly most affected by this are those who have special physical needs. In addition, in the future, we can only speculate about how this will affect transport systems, the climate, and urban areas. Slowly but surely, our experiences will draw perceptual impressions from the Internet, which is being increasingly based on artificial intelligence and intelligent robots (Johannessen, 2020). Our experiences are increasingly connected to a growing and more intelligent cyberspace. So it is not just our bodies that experience a "new" world, but also our cognitive functions. Our bodies, with their limitations, and our cognitive functions, are entering a new world of experience made possible by the new technological and organizational innovations. In the future, the same can also be imagined to happen with our emotions (Johannessen, 2021).

Our ability to organize our businesses, institutions, and society has no limits. However, we are perhaps limited by certain ideas, such as the idea that profit comes before people's welfare. The point of reflecting on putting profit before people's welfare is to show that we can organize ourselves so that it promotes everyone in society, not just the few. The technology in the Fourth Industrial Revolution has the possibility of liberating the body's limitations, especially for those with disabilities, but also for other people. Our ability to organize ourselves is unlimited. We are only limited by our own ideological systems.

In the phenomenology of embodiment, the lived body is our lived centre of experience. We can thus also liberate ourselves, if not from our bodies, but by making our bodies less dependent on being located at a specific workplace. The human body is limited in various ways. It is especially people with disabilities who can feel constrained and limited by their bodies. However, the new technology in the Fourth Industrial Revolution will be able to help individuals with disabilities in various ways, so it is unlikely they will oppose this development.

Proposition: The innovations of the Fourth Industrial Revolution will reduce many of the limitations that prevent people with disabilities from being socially included in working life.

Practical utility related to innovation and productivity

People with disabilities belong to a minority group. In her book, *The Minority Body* (2016), Elizabeth Barnes proposes that disability is not a physical or mental category but a socially constructed category. In other words, in a society that focuses on productivity those people who are not able to fully participate in production are viewed as not being "normal," and are thus discriminated against in many ways, such as in relation to the labour market. Barnes argues that being physically disabled is not to have a defective body, but to have a minority body, and disabled people are discriminated against on the grounds of their minority status, like other types of minority discrimination based on race, gender, age, and so on. For example, being old is not a disease. If older people perform their work better than many young people, why should they be deprived by law of the right to work; in other words, because an institutionalized norm dictates it. Similarly, institutionalized norms discriminate against people with minority bodies, and other minorities, because they are "not like" the majority. Viewing people with disabilities as a minority is a social construction, and consequently also a social "problem." Many older people look forward to retirement so they can stop working. However, many others wish to continue working but are unable to do so because they have reached a mandatory retirement age. This may be viewed as a type of institutional discrimination. In other words, many older people are prevented from working not because they are unable to work, but because they fall outside the boundaries of an institutionalized norm.

Thus, having a "minority body" is a social construction. Many people wear glasses and are sometimes perceived as having a "handicap," but this view is not necessarily shared by those who wear the glasses. Similarly, wheelchair users are perceived as being disabled, whereas, the wheelchair user will not necessarily share this view. It is often thought that older people should be "grateful" that they are "allowed" to work. In other words, they have to go cap in hand and constantly adapt to the boss's whims.

People who wear large hats have to be careful when moving around amongst people. It might be said that they belong to a "minority." However, when they take off their hat they cease to be a "minority," and become like everyone else without hats. However, people with "minority bodies" cannot do the same and just become like everyone else. Wheelchair users have a visible "disability," yet may do their work just as well as others. In this case, why should they be discriminated against because they have a "minority body"? The answer is simple, disabled people are discriminated against on the grounds of their minority status. Surely no one will object to the fact that excavators are used to dig ditches! It takes approximately 20–30 men to dig a ditch as fast as an excavator. Do you then belong to a minority just because a machine can work quicker and better than you can? Of course not. Do you belong to a minority if you are disabled, and someone who is not disabled is able to work, let's say, 30 per cent better and faster than you can? Yes, many would say. What if we reverse this situation. If someone with a "minority body" works 100 per cent better and faster than someone without a disability, does the person who works more slowly belong to a minority? No, few, if any, would say. The point here is that having a disability or a "minority body" is a socially constructed phenomenon. It is the phenomenon in itself that is discriminated against, not necessarily the person concerned. That's why those who discriminate against others often say: "It's not about you!" Who is it about then?

Sub-conclusion related to innovation and productivity

In this section, we have examined the following question: How can innovation and productivity affect the employment of people with disabilities?

People with disabilities are able to use various equipment and technological aids, such as, wheelchairs, hearing and vision aids, artificial limbs and communication aids; this enables them to function better in their environments. In the near future, people in general will also increasingly use technological aids to enable them to function and communicate better. For example, computerized glasses are already being developed by many tech companies. In the future, other types of innovations will also be able to assist many people with "minority bodies," such as the categories referred to above in Figure 5.8; this will enable them to improve their well-being and their working lives. The assumption here is that the innovations that will emerge in the Fourth Industrial Revolution will make it easier for people with disabilities to find work. In this way, it can be said that the concepts of "minority body" and technology are closely linked. In particular, this will apply to AI and body technology.

Main conclusion

In this chapter, we have examined the following general research question: How can artificial intelligence and intelligent robots affect the employment of people with disabilities in organizations?

Human strength does not lie in the body, but in the ability to create tools, which can be used to make everyday life easier. For people with disabilities, this is especially the case, as they often need technical devices of one kind or another, in order to fully function. The point here is that people with "minority bodies" and technology are systemically linked with regard to innovations. When the visually impaired, the hard of hearing, the physically challenged, or the cognitively challenged are in need of support they are often dependent on technological innovations, in order to function better. In other words, in this context, there is a strong connection between people with disabilities and technological innovations.

When the Singularity occurs around 2035–2040, people with "minority bodies" and other people with disabilities will probably be the ones who benefit most from new innovations, because their disabilities will be largely offset by the new technological devices.

During the First Industrial Revolution, the Luddite weavers opposed new technological developments in the form of the weaving machines, which stole their jobs.[17] Today, the Neo-Luddites are opposing the unregulated development of AI and robotics. Technological innovations were first used to replace human physical

1. Technology relieves humans from physical toil	**4. Technology as a support for creative activities**
2. Technology eliminates repetitive work	**3. Technology helps people with cognitive challenges**

Figure 5.11 The "Technology Window."

toil. Later, new technological innovations were used to replace routine and repetitive work. When the Singularity occurs, new innovations will not only benefit people with "minority bodies," but everyone who works with repetitive, and often meaningless, tasks.

The short answer to the general research question is that the symbiosis between "minority bodies" and technology will open up new opportunities in working life for people with disabilities. Amongst other things, it is very probable that new technology will be developed that can assist people who are cognitively challenged. In addition, there is much evidence that new technology will be developed that can function as a support for creative activities. The "Technology Window" in Figure 5.11 shows the various ways in which technology will be of use.

Notes

1 Nusbaum (2011:211–230) includes a list of works that are based on this knowledge perspective. This perspective is also described and analysed in Austin (2019); Gangas (2019); and Dalziel and Saunders (2019). The Human Development Approach is closely related to the United Nations Development Program (UNDP) report, which has been published annually since 1990.

2 Our scientific and theoretical approach is based on Mario Bunge's work. Please refer to the references in the bibliography of this chapter.

3 Technology is here understood as "the scientific study of artefacts" (Bunge, 1985: 219-231).

4 Rose uses the modern term "disability" when discussing this group of people in the Greco-Roman world. However, there were no Latin or Greek words for "disabled." The Romans used the word "monstrum" (mythical monster), while the Greeks used the term "adunatos" (unable). Thus, the author's use of the modern term "disability" at times confuses the reader in what is otherwise excellent research.

5 This refers to "lepers, the blind, the dumb, the deaf, the natural fool, the cripple, the lame and the lunatic" (Slorach, 2016: 53).

6 The first edition of Newton's book, *Principia,* was published in 1687. https://en.wikipedia.org/wiki/Age_of_Enlightenment

7 The First Industrial Revolution, which began around 1750 was driven by the steam engine; the Second Industrial Revolution, which began around 1870 was driven by the internal combustion engine, electricity, and mass production; and the Third Industrial Revolution, which began around the 1950s was driven by the rise of digital technology

and the Internet. The Fourth Industrial Revolution will be characterized by robotics, artificial intelligence, and related technologies (2035–2040) (Kurtzweil, 2005; 2008; Johannessen, 2020).

8 The division is based on systemic thinking, as described in Mario Bunge (2003).

9 The generation born between 1981 and 1996.

10 https://en.wikipedia.org/wiki/Millennials

11 GRIT refers to people who are passionate about their work, and who are persistent in achieving long-term goals.

12 https://www.theguardian.com/environment/2019/sep/02/greta-thunberg-responds-to-aspergers-critics-its-a-superpower

13 This does not include the world's poor.

14 AI Singularity is a future event in which artificial intelligence will have surpassed human intelligence.

15 https://www.theguardian.com/environment/greta-thunberg

16 https://en.wikipedia.org/wiki/Maurice_Merleau-Ponty

17 https://en.wikipedia.org/wiki/Luddite

6 Discrimination in the workplace against people with disabilities

Key points

- In this chapter, we have identified three categories of discrimination.
- Within each category, we have identified four specific types of discrimination.
- In all, we describe, analyse and make theoretical and practical observations about 12 strategies for tackling discrimination in the workplace.

Introduction

Discrimination brings about social change. At first sight, this statement seems paradoxical. The point we are making, however, is that in the longer term, discriminatory practices are likely to cause a backlash that ultimately will bring about an end to such practices. We have seen examples of such processes in several countries that have now enacted laws to prevent discrimination against people with disabilities.

Disabled people experience discrimination in a number of ways. One should reflect on which values one advocates when using the various discrimination strategies against disabled people. In this chapter, we will describe and analyse three different categories of discrimination against people with disabilities. These are active discrimination, passive discrimination, and "making people invisible."

Active discrimination

The most direct discrimination can be called active discrimination. The different types of active discrimination can be social exclusion, institutionalization, and regulation by law.

The way people with disabilities are defined, the models used, and the discrimination strategies used, consciously or unconsciously, are based on certain norms and values. Establishing these norms and values explicitly clarifies the basis for people's thinking in relation to people with disabilities in working life. If a medical phenomenon is viewed as being a type of disease, then this becomes contrasted with people who are healthy. The question then arises is, "Can sick people work?" The guidelines established in relation to this way of thinking form the framework for the actions people take.

DOI: 10.4324/9781003497325-8

Passive discrimination

Another form of discrimination can be called passive discrimination. This can include social exclusion, micro-discrimination, or "looking away" in a meeting. To "look away" must not be confused with overlooking. When you "look away," you are not overlooking, but are in a subtle way active in ignoring people.

The idea that those people with disabilities will be difficult to employ is in itself an active discrimination strategy. This discrimination strategy is immanent in the idea that people have to function perfectly and have no disabilities if they are to be useful to production. Being able to walk independently without an aid seems to be an important prerequisite for being considered fit for work. Workplaces need to be more accessible for employees with mobility impairments. Workplaces that are not designed to allow this, exclude and discriminate passively against workers with such impairments (Oliver, 2009: 27–40).

Making people "invisible" and discrimination

The third discrimination strategy is rendering people "invisible." A special type of "invisibility," as a discrimination strategy, is that one feels that one's value as a human being is depreciated, because one is not able to perform work in the same way as most others. One of the effects for those people who are exposed to this type of discrimination is that their self-identity is damaged. Another way of making disabled people "invisible" is not taking seriously what they say. Another type in the same category is when people's facial expression says "It's hopeless," or they show exasperation. A subcategory of making people "invisible" is to overlook them. Being overlooked is often perceived as offensive. This discrimination strategy appears when people respond with a smirk, and when they adopt the attitude that people need to fend for themselves and not be a burden to others. This category also appears in the attitude that signals "Oh no, not him again!."

Part of the "invisibility" strategy is to define people with disability by using an "individual model," where it is the individual who is focused on, i.e., the problems faced by the disabled person, resulting from their impairment, and thus also the help they need. In 1981, organizations for the disabled adopted the social model and rejected the individual model. Mike Oliver coined the phrase "The Social Model of Disability" (Fougeyrollas & Beauregard, 2001: 177). The social model focuses on the fact that disability is something imposed on top of people's impairments by the way they are unnecessarily isolated and excluded from workplaces, and participation in society (Shakespeare & Watson, 1997: 293–300). In other words, it is how society is organized that is disabling, not a person's disability.

Part of the strategy of discriminating against people with disabilities is choosing to ignore that a problem exists. In 1964, the US Congress passed the Civil Rights Act, which prohibited discrimination on the basis of race, colour, religion, sex, or national origin. However, the Civil Rights Act did not mention disabled people, although the Act was later expanded to include this group. In other words, the passing of the Act in 1964 was tantamount to overlooking a large group of Americans, which, at the time, had an adverse effect on the possibility of employment for people with disabilities (Patterson, 2018: 448).

In this chapter, we will examine the following general research question: *How are people with disabilities discriminated against in working life?*

In order to address the general research question, we have formulated the three following research questions:

1. What kinds of active discrimination affect people with disabilities in the workplace?
2. What kinds of passive discrimination affect people with disabilities in the workplace?
3. How are people with disabilities discriminated against in the workplace by being rendered "invisible"?

The introduction is shown figuratively in Figure 6.1, which also shows how this chapter is organized.

Active discrimination

In this section, we examine the following question: What kinds of active discrimination affect people with disabilities in the workplace?

Although disability research has come a long way, there is relatively little research that has focused on the various discrimination strategies towards people with disabilities (Shakespeare, 2015). In other words, there are gaps in the

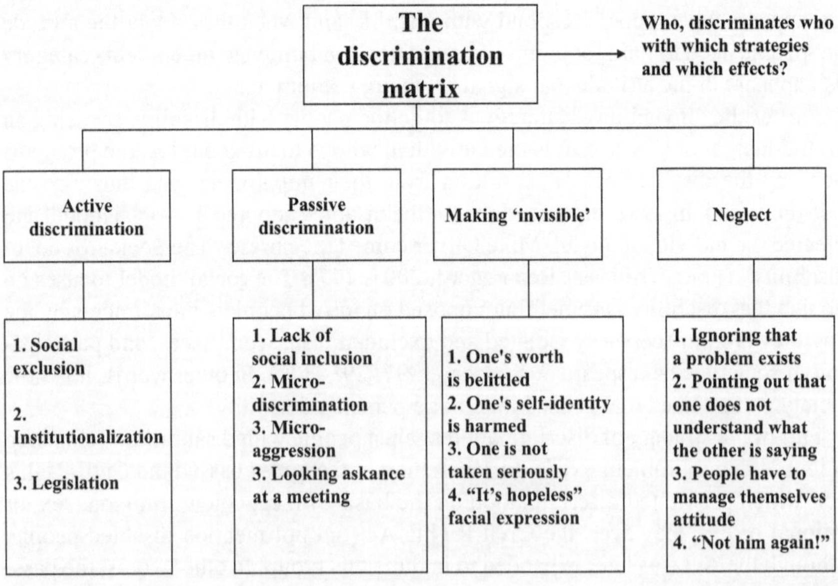

Figure 6.1 The discrimination matrix.

knowledge about how society reacts towards different discrimination strategies. Both conceptual and empirical contributions that can fill this knowledge gap can also influence policy towards this group.

Three of the active discrimination strategies that have had a negative impact on people with disabilities are social exclusion, institutionalization and legal regulation (Ravaud & Stiker, 2001: 490). Allowing or not allowing some people to create their own relationships through work says something about a country's culture and about the management of workplaces. As a general rule, one can claim that social exclusion is often motivated by good intentions to help those concerned. The French abbot, Bernard of Clairvaux (1090–1153), said that "The Road to Hell is Paved with Good Intentions."[1] In such a context, we might rewrite his statement in the following way: "So-called 'good intentions' are collected in buckets and pails on 'refuse dumps', in order to be socially recycled again and again." If one examines the origin of social exclusion of people with disabilities, this will not be found explicitly in political agendas and policies, because such policies are formulated as positive intentions, even if the consequences for those concerned are negative. What you often hear from the political authorities is, as a general rule, that they were unable to include as many people as they wanted, and that they need more time. However, this raises a question: If intentions do not lead to the desired results, what is needed to include people with disabilities in working life? Those with disabilities are thus actively discriminated against, although intentions are formulated as "social inclusion."

Description related to active discrimination

Active discrimination has two extremes. One extreme is the eradication of certain social groups that are viewed as being a burden to society. In 1939, the German Nazi regime launched its T-4 Program. About 375,000 people with disabilities were sterilized. It is estimated that by the end of the war 275,000 people with congenital disabilities were murdered.[2]

Another form of active exclusion is to isolate people with disabilities, the so-called institutionalization, which restricts the freedom of disabled persons by preventing association with the rest of the society. Such institutions are often situated in rural and isolated areas, so they are "out-of-sight." Another form of active exclusion is to isolate and discriminate against people with disabilities economically, socially, and politically. For example, when people with disabilities do not receive the necessary care they need. This occurs in countries where health services are not a human right, but based on insurance schemes. Those who do not have the necessary insurance will thus not receive the care and attention they need.

Active discrimination is culturally and legally conditioned. The economic exclusion related to culture is often based on norms that have been established in the culture over a period of time. In some cultures, caring for the disabled is a social responsibility. In other cultures, caring for the disabled and the aged is a family responsibility. In yet other cultures, the care of the disabled is based on privately

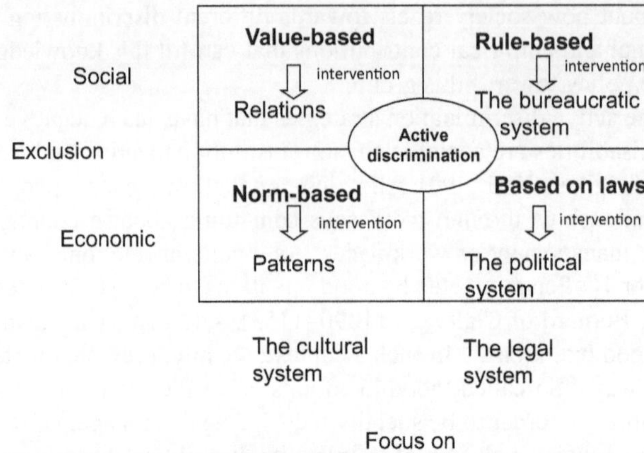

Figure 6.2 Typology of active discrimination.

financed health insurance schemes. Regardless of how the care is organized, it is norm-based. In other words, social exclusion is norm-based within the various cultures. Regardless of the outcome, social exclusion is thus value-based.

The economic exclusion of people with disabilities is often enshrined in the legal system, i.e., regulated by law. The specification of such laws will depend on the context and culture, as well as the type of disability. The legal system may not specifically adopt a law for social exclusion, but the exclusion may be based on the interaction of various regulations and rules.

Active discrimination is a form of marginalization, where social and economic exclusion is used in different ways, but where the desired result is the same; exclusion from working life. The reasons given may be described in positive terms, but the social and economic consequences are always the same, exclusion from working life and other social contexts.

All the four types of active discrimination we have mentioned in Figure 6.2 have one thing in common: marginalization. Through active discrimination, those with disabilities are marginalized in one way or another. We have in Figure 6.2 shown suggestions for what interventions can be made in relation to the various types of active discrimination, in order to reduce marginalization. These are only intended as suggestions, to show that active discrimination can also be subject to change.

Analysis related to active discrimination

Figure 6.2 focuses on the social and economic aspects of active discrimination. The general research question in this chapter asks: How are people with disabilities discriminated against in working life? When disabled people are excluded from working life, they are also excluded socially, and disadvantaged economically. Much research has been carried out in relation to this problem complex (Heyman et al., 2014). In the past, there was a clear connection between physical disabilities and discrimination strategies in working life (Oliver, 1990). Today, there is a greater focus on the local culture and the local surroundings, related to how these can facilitate work opportunities for people with various disabilities, such as physical or cognitive disabilities, who need special help in order to function satisfactorily. This focus came largely as a result of the UN's Convention on the Rights of Persons with Disabilities (UN, 2006). In other words, the focus today is more on how to break down barriers in the local environment, and to reduce and remove obstacles for people with disabilities. The UN and other authorities are attempting to influence changes in legislation, and to prevent social and economic exclusion. Today, we have the following information about the social and economic situation of people with disabilities (Macdonald, 2015: 123–126):

- The majority of persons with disabilities live in conditions of poverty.
- Children with disabilities are more likely than non-disabled children to be victims of abuse.
- Children with disabilities are much more likely than non-disabled children to be victims of sexual violence.
- Children with disabilities are often abandoned by their parents.
- Children with disabilities are more likely than non-disabled children to run away from home.
- Children with disabilities are more likely to be homeless than non-disabled children.
- Children with disabilities are much more likely to be bullied at school than their non-disabled peers.
- Children with disability are more likely to suffer from depression and angst than their non-disabled peers.
- Families with disabled children are more likely to live in poverty.

Of course, we could continue with this list, but the point being made here is that laws and regulations need to be changed in order to help this group; this would represent the first step towards preventing active discrimination. Intervention is also necessary to improve local cultures, so that norms and values are changed in a positive direction. Without changing local cultures, there will still be obstacles, so that it will be difficult to reduce active discrimination significantly. Having said this, the UN Convention, and the legislation in many countries that prohibit discrimination against various groups, such as people with disabilities, will function as a social mechanism for facilitating collective responsibility, which will be of great importance to people with disabilities, especially in relation to being able to enter working life.

Theoretical points related to active discrimination

Is indifference a form of active discrimination? For example, we know from research that people with dyslexia are, in many contexts, more determined, creative, and productive than those without dyslexia (Rooke, 2016; 2018). On the other hand, it is unlikely that HR departments take this knowledge into account in their employment strategy when they need people who have these qualities, i.e., determined, creative, and productive. Dyslexia is often referred to as the invisible disability, because you are unable to see it.

On the other hand, in most western countries, it is illegal to discriminate against people with disabilities in working life. For example, the United Kingdom passed the Disability Discrimination Act in 1995, protecting disabled people against various types of discrimination (Borsay, 2005: 1). However, the law was not precise enough in its formulation for those who did not have a visible disability, such as dyslexia; consequently, the law did not adequately cover discrimination against people with dyslexia. People with dyslexia in the United States have not been adequately protected by the law regarding discrimination; consequently, they often end up in a situation where they are unable to support themselves. Studies have shown that people with dyslexia are overrepresented within the homeless population (Macdonald, 2015: 112–132). In other words, they are physically socially excluded (Macdonald, 2015: 117–118). People with dyslexia often perform poorly within the education system, and are sometimes labelled as "less gifted." Consequently, they often do not have the education and skills that are demanded in the labour market, and thus suffer economically (Macdonald, 2015). The good side of the coin is that those who manage to meet the demands of the school system and the labour market will become the new hard-working, creative, and innovative people we need at the entrance to the Fourth Industrial Revolution (Rooke, 2016; 2018).

The laws that were passed after the Second World War to protect people with disabilities against discrimination often did not cover all types of disabilities. For example, those disabilities that are "invisible," such as dyslexia. This resulted in many people with dyslexia being subjected to active discrimination (Macdonald, 2015: 112–132).

Proposition: Many people with "invisible" disabilities are discriminated against, especially in the labour market.

Practical utility related to active discrimination

Disability is a social construction. At first glance, this statement seems to be a paradox. How can soldiers who return home from wars with their limbs shot off be a social construction? The point of the statement is that it is how society treats people with disabilities that is a social construction. As a society, we can choose to discriminate against people with disabilities, or we can choose to include them in working life. It is this process that lies inherent in the statement that disability is a social construction. Doctors may diagnose a disability; however, the word "disability" can also be used in social or legal contexts. People may also feel strongly that they have a disability, but this personal experience is distinguished from the medical, social, and legal meanings of the word. In a social context, we say that disability is socially constructed, because society has a moral responsibility to ensure that people with disabilities can function socially, and in working life, and have the same rights as people without disabilities.

Historically speaking, in the Western world, disability has been mainly linked to visible disabilities. Thus, those with "invisible" disabilities are still often actively discriminated against in working life. However, it seems that this discrimination is mainly based on ignorance, rather than a desire to actively discriminate. If ignorance is the main reason behind such discrimination, then researchers and politicians have a joint responsibility to increase the level of awareness regarding people with "invisible" disabilities, so that this leads to improving the employment opportunities for this group of people. At a time when new technology will compensate for much of the so-called "invisible" disabilities, an increase in the level of awareness regarding "invisible" disabilities will benefit all parties.

Much of the research, regarding the question being discussed here, of how active discrimination affects people with disabilities in the workplace, focuses on the disadvantages of being disabled, and what can be done to ease disabled people's situation in working and social life. However what if we phrase this question differently? How can organizations and society benefit from employing people with disabilities? Could the answer be as simple that by changing our perspective, we will be able to learn from such a process? A change of perspective can help us to see various phenomena and problems from other sides, and thus create an opening for creative and innovative ideas. Changing perspective is a way of learning how to think outside the box.

Sub-conclusion related to active discrimination

In this section, we have discussed the following question: What kinds of active discrimination affect people with disabilities in the workplace?

In today's society, people who have been medically diagnosed as having a disability, which is covered by laws against discrimination, are less exposed to active discrimination. These people will be able to claim their legal right to employment and be able to enter the labour market. It is largely those people with "invisible" disabilities, such as dyslexia, who are actively discriminated against in the labour market.

Passive discrimination

In this section, we will examine the following question: What kinds of passive discrimination affect people with disabilities in the workplace?

Lack of social inclusion, looking askance at a meeting, as well as other forms of micro-discrimination, are examples of passive discrimination. Micro-discrimination is the many small signals that are sent but are difficult to understand by anyone other than those for whom the signals are intended. This can be raised eyebrows, shaking your head in resignation, sighing to express negativity, and so on. For those who experience this micro-discrimination, a clear and distinct message is sent. Micro-discrimination differs from micro-aggression[3] in that micro-discrimination is perceived discrimination, while micro-aggression is real rejection.

It is often the social barriers to entering social contexts, which are a form of passive discrimination. Since the 1970s, the physical barriers that disabled people might experience when accessing locations and services have largely been removed, such as steps and stairways, and so on. Today, it is not the physical barriers that are a problem, but micro-discrimination and a lack of social inclusion, which is a type of passive discrimination. It is the effects of passive discrimination that we are concerned with here. Micro-discrimination and micro-aggression are two sides of the same coin. While micro-aggression can apply to many phenomena, here we use the term micro-discrimination to refer specifically to discrimination against people with disabilities. Micro-discrimination is often aimed at a specific person, or against a whole group of people, e.g., the elderly (ageism). When the offender is confronted with this form of micro-discrimination, the answer is often: "It doesn't apply to you, you know." This is a form of inclusive sociality that is on par with the so-called good intentions that pave the road away from positive inclusive social relations.

Narratives related to passive discrimination

Case letter 1: The misuse of words such as "cripple," "handicapped," "imbecile," and "invalid" can have a negative impact, resulting in discrimination

Words have meanings both for the people they refer to and for the people who use them. If someone is described as "a cripple," this implies that they are "defective." Although measures can be taken to compensate for their "defects," they will never be fully functional. In contrast, if we say that the work environment at Company A is defective and has too many physical barriers for people with disabilities to function effectively, then our perspective on the situation is completely turned around. Thus, it is not the individual who is "defective," because they have one or more disabilities, but the organization's operating conditions that are unsatisfactory. If a company says that person X's disabilities make it financially unviable for the company to employ them, then the company is taking the position that the responsibility for social exclusion rests on the person with disabilities, rather than on the company. It is in this kind of context that we see examples of micro-discriminations. For example, people will often say that they "understand" the situation, they mean well, they have positive intentions, but regrettably they are subject to certain operating conditions that they cannot ignore. Micro-discriminations are often framed in a positive way, but they have a negative outcome for the person being discriminated against.

Description related to passive discrimination

Today, active and passive discrimination are not linked to segregation policies, as was the case in the past (Borsay, 2005). Passive discrimination is more subtle than active discrimination, but the consequences are the same. The positive tone that can often be heard in micro-discrimination, and the lack of social integration, result in social exclusion. Micro-discrimination can be on a very specific level. When a group of people have a reading circle, certain people may not be included for various reasons. When a dining club excludes certain people, it may be argued that "unfortunately there is no room." This is micro-discrimination in everyday life. However, the person who is excluded will have a feeling of being rejected. The signals sent, regardless of the rational explanation and positive tone of the rejection, are experienced by the person in question as social exclusion.

Even if there is a positive undertone in the other's behaviour, there may be a low level of social inclusion. This may confirm that one does not mean anything to the other person or group. Lack of social inclusion applies, as a general rule, to a group of people, e.g., those with disabilities, ethnic groups, special groups of immigrants, etc.

Passive discrimination can also be signalled by a negative tone. One type of this behaviour is the averted gaze. This is not the same as being "overlooked," but rather being seen, but disregarded. There is a large difference between being overlooked and being seen, but ignored. The person who discriminates can claim that he/she has done nothing actively and thus has not discriminated against anyone. It can be argued that discrimination, involving an "averted gaze," is a special form of passive discrimination, and not an active form of discrimination. However, both active and passive discrimination are forms of communication. One cannot communicate in communicative situations. The congratulations you forgot to send your wife on your 25th wedding anniversary is also a form of communication. The lack of communication is actually communicating that "you don't care."

In other words, micro-aggression is a term used for everyday verbal and behavioural slights, whether intentional or unintentional, that communicates negative attitudes towards marginalized groups – in our context, disabled people. The term was first coined by the American psychiatrist Chester M. Pierce in 1970 to describe the insults which he regularly witnessed non-black Americans inflicting on African Americans.[4] In recent decades, the term has been applied to the casual disparagement suffered by other marginalized groups, such as mentioned, disabled people. As also mentioned above, this type of passive discrimination can be expressed by a smirk, the shrugging of shoulders, the raising of eyebrows, a sigh of resignation, an averted gaze, and so on.

Analysis related to passive discrimination

Passive discrimination can function in such a way that certain people are viewed as being "defective," and consequently, they need to be removed or isolated from the rest of society, so they do not "contaminate" those people without any "defects." Of course, those people who passively discriminate others would never vouch for such a definition. On the contrary, they will mainly talk in a positive tone, and have an "understanding" attitude, while regretting that it is not possible to do anything about social inclusion at this point in time, saying, "Later maybe, but unfortunately not yet."

The point is that it will never be possible to carry out this social inclusion, because one actually regards the other person(s) as socially "defective," as someone who will "contaminate" their social environment and impose an aesthetic value on their relationships that they really don't want. There is the exception where those with disabilities are included in the social community, which is characterized by passive discrimination. Beneath this idea of passive discrimination lies the idea of normalization, i.e., what is "defective" needs to be restored, so that it does not "contaminate" in any way. In other words, the focus here is on the individual, the person with disabilities, not on a socially- created reality that defines "disability" in relation to economic productive forces. That is to say, underlying the active and passive discrimination is the idea that people need to be productive, and add value to the economy. If one does not add value, then one is considered to be unproductive rather than productive; in other words, he/she only consumes what others have produced. The above thinking relates to neoliberal capitalism which poses the idea that people should be productive, an idea which negatively affects people with disabilities (Mitchell & Snyder, 2015: 204–222). The cultural idea that emerges from such an ideology is that people with disabilities are a burden on society. If someone is perceived as a burden, then such a cultural attitude fosters a climate of passive discrimination, even if those people who passively discriminate others perceive themselves as being inclusive and positive towards people who need help. The idea that some people are a burden to society is closely linked to various forms of discrimination, especially in a society that underlines people's economic productivity. In other words, unproductive people are a burden to productive people. It is the use of the thought model that some people are productive, while those who are unproductive are parasitic, and only consume what is produced by others, which ultimately leads to various forms of passive discrimination.

What happens when we divide people into "the productive" and "the unproductive parasitic consumers," is that we create an arena where it is "us and them" that becomes the central distinction. They are the "others," the "strangers," the ones we must be careful about including in our culture. Although we may allow a small degree of social inclusion, we must show them by our behaviour and attitudes that they are strangers to our culture, they do not belong here, they are different, and do not fit in. This behaviour and attitude can emerge as "the averted gaze," micro-discrimination and micro-aggression, and so on.

Theoretical points related to passive discrimination

Passive discrimination is not necessarily a system of conscious discrimination. It is possible that it is only micro-aggression that signals wilful rejection. The other types in the typology in Figure 6.3 are of a more veiled form of discrimination. Perceived rejection may represent a strong type of discrimination, but it is not certain that the person concerned becomes aware of this form of rejection until a special event creates the necessary insight. One could say that passive discrimination disciplines more than it oppresses. Few people want to experience not being socially included or have the feeling that they are being rejected. Therefore, behaviour is changed,

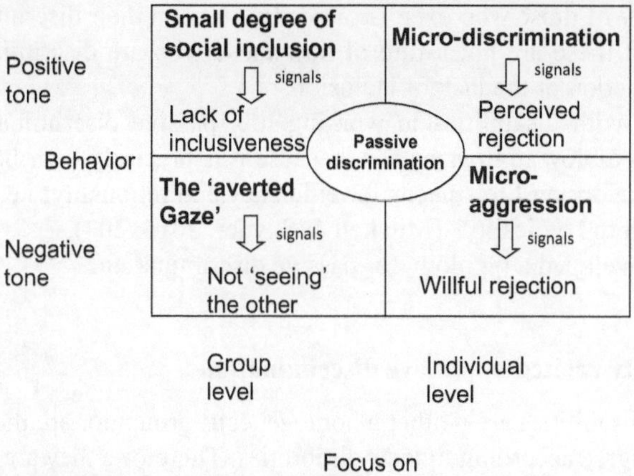

Figure 6.3 Typology of passive discrimination.

so that these types of passive discrimination are not enforced. In this way, passive discrimination disciplines, so that the other party does not have to use this form of discrimination. In other words, passive discrimination is often an attempt at "disciplining" the other party.

While active discrimination can be viewed as a type of "dynamo" that creates energy for social and economic exclusion, passive discrimination is more at the level of suggestion. Passive discrimination is a feeling that exists, but it is not active. However, it can be activated if the person being potentially discriminated against does not adjust his/her behaviour according to what the discrimination suggests. The social dimension that lies in the behavioural regulation of passive discrimination cannot be overlooked, because it focuses on the discriminated person's way of relating to others.

When people have experienced various types of passive discrimination over a long period of time, it seems reasonable to assume that they will adjust their behaviour, so that the discrimination is not further enforced. You can choose strategies such as making yourself smaller, becoming "invisible," repressing your true personality, or meeting the stereotype others have of you. In this way, you take the sting out of the discrimination, and turn it away from yourself. In other words, you cultivate a form of mirroring, where you do not come under the spotlight of the discrimination.

Proposition: Passive discrimination disciplines the behaviour of those being potentially discriminated against.

Passive discrimination differs from active discrimination in its way of operating, but both types of discrimination, passive and active, in their consequences, are experienced as being excluded from the community. However, an important difference must be emphasized. It is not entirely clear whether those who engage in passive discrimination are aware of the fact that they are discriminating. This applies to many of those who exercise a positive tone in their discrimination strategies. Many of these are not aware of how those who are discriminated against experience rejection or the lack of inclusion.

For people with disabilities in working life, passive discrimination is often experienced as a blow to their bodies, because it is precisely their bodies that are not adapted to working life's needs for efficiency and rationality; i.e., their bodies do not conform to "typicality" (Mitchell & Snyder, 2015: 204).

We have developed a typology for passive discrimination.

Practical utility related to passive discrimination

Persons with disabilities are neither a homogeneous group nor are they segregated to any great degree according to their disabilities. Therefore, they are not discriminated against in the same way either. Passive discrimination is therefore experienced very differently for the various social groups to which those people with disabilities belong. What the disabled have in common is that they have a minority body. The point is simply that having a minority body is not the only factor that determines the level of discrimination. To elaborate, it is likely that those persons who have a high social status will experience passive discrimination in a different way than those who have a low social status.

Passive discrimination may also be viewed in relation to the degree of functional disability. The aesthetics of disability relates to the visible behavioural markers that trigger aesthetic and affective judgments towards people with disability,

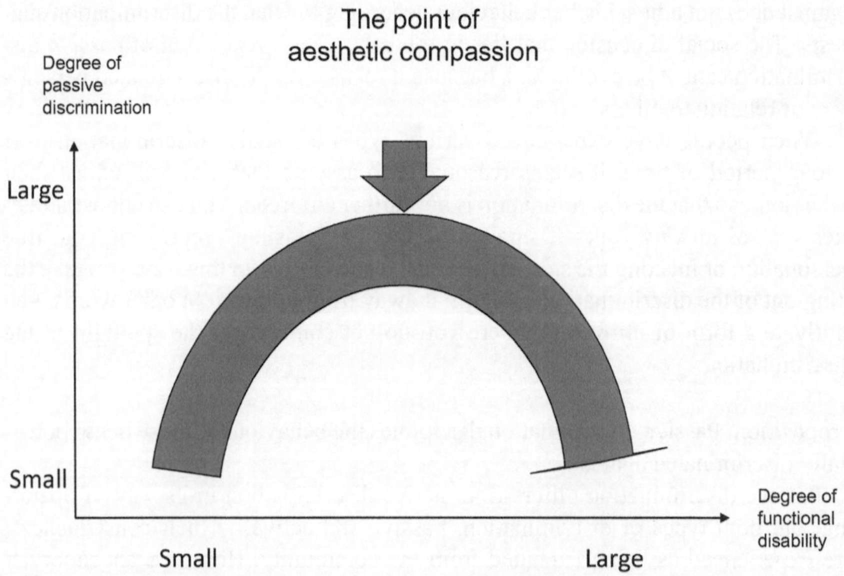

Figure 6.4 Discrimination and the degree of functional disability.

also in relation to the degree of functional disability people have. In this context, one can say that passive discrimination rises with the degree of functional disability. However, when the discrimination and the level of functional disability reach a certain point in an inverted U, then the point of aesthetic compassion occurs, and the level of discrimination falls in relation to increased functional disability, as shown in Figure 6.4.

Sub-conclusion related to passive discrimination

In this section, we have examined the following question: What kinds of passive discrimination affect people with disabilities in the workplace?

Passive discrimination against people with disabilities in working life may be viewed as occurring along two main axes. One axis is based on a positive fundamental tone. Even if the basic tone is positive, the individual will experience this discrimination as rejection, even if this was not necessarily the intention. The group as such experiences a lack of social inclusion, even if the basic tone is positive. As a psychological phenomenon, this is experienced as a lack of confirmation of one's usefulness or value as an employee.

The second axis highlights a negative tone in relation to discrimination. Here, the individual experiences this as a wilful and real rejection, which can be described as a form of micro-aggression. Disabled people experience this form of negative tone as not being "seen," where the one discriminating uses an "averted gaze," and an attitude expressing hopelessness. When you are not "seen" or appreciated it is worse than being overlooked, because you question your own value, which can undermine your self-esteem and impair motivation in the workplace.

Rendering people "invisible"

In this section, we will examine the following question: How are people with disabilities discriminated against in the workplace by being rendered "invisible"?

What do you see when you see a disabled person? Do you see their disability first, and the person second? Most people probably see the disability first and not the person. We can take this observation a little further. If someone with a disability manages to out-compete a person without any visible disability for a position in a business, what do we think? Most people will probably think that the person with a disability got the job, because according to the law, businesses are obliged to employ a certain number of people with disabilities.

Narratives related to "invisibility"

Case letter 1: Our experience and social interactions shape our frame of reference

The limitations of people with disabilities make them who they are. Their experiences and social interactions have created their frames of reference. This is not a discriminatory statement, but something that is based on what people with disabilities themselves say. If people are shaped into something other than what they perceive themselves to be, then this can sometimes be explained by the social interactions that render them "invisible." It is precisely the limitations that set the boundaries for disabled people's world of experience. Choosing to ignore these limitations is the same as trying to change their self-understanding. It is often claimed that one overlooks the disabled person's limitations in order to be kind and inclusive. However, this is also a way of ignoring something that everyone is aware of. For example, if a person uses a wheelchair at work, the wheelchair is of course part of their world of experience. Ignoring such an important thing may be likened to overlooking an important part of the person's life.

Description related to "invisibility"

Tolerance and understanding are not the same. It is possible to tolerate or accept a person without understanding him or her. If, on the other hand, you understand and share another person's experiences, then you have empathy for the other person's situation, and will discriminate against the person to a lesser extent. Tolerance of people with disabilities can be viewed as a special form of charity (Read, 2000: 33), and is a special variant of discrimination, where you may negatively influence the other's self-understanding.

Disabled people can be discriminated against in relation to both physical and social barriers. The "invisibility" lies in rejecting that this is discrimination; e.g., one may say that it is not possible to remove a physical barrier due to the high costs of making architectural changes. For instance, when the elevator does not go to the sixth floor, thus preventing disabled access for wheelchair users. However, whatever the reason, this will be perceived as discrimination. Physical barriers are often systemically linked to social barriers. If the workplace's creative energy mainly occurs on the sixth floor, then the disabled person is excluded from this, regardless of the explanations.

Even if attitudes towards people with disabilities have changed in a positive direction, rendering them "invisible" will seem discriminatory. People with minority bodies are not openly laughed at, but ignoring that they have certain limitations is a form of discrimination that degrades the other, because the experiences that have shaped them are overlooked.

Analysis related to "invisibility"

Disability is socially constructed and perpetuates the oppression of people with minority bodies. In other words, people are "disabled" by social barriers, and not by their impairment. The question is whether this will change in the Fourth Industrial Revolution, where artificial intelligence and robotics can remedy many of the challenges associated with minority bodies.

The oppressive and discriminatory attitudes associated with disability, which makes people with disabilities "invisible," are closely linked to ideology, i.e., to the prevailing ideas and dominant logic in society. If the prevailing ideology is linked to productivity, profit, and economic growth, then it is easy to understand that the ideology will be directed towards error-free products, error-free processes, and error-free inputs in the processes. In such thinking, anyone with disabilities may easily fall outside the productive logic. Having said this, we have also linked disability with the social system. In a solidarity economy, based on cooperation and democratic ethics, this will not be a problem. On the other hand, a type of capitalism which is based on profit maximization and the downscaling of costs, in order to increase the profits for shareholders, will represent a large problem for people with disabilities. This applies to people with minority bodies, dyslexia, ADHD, Asperger's Syndrome, and the elderly, and everyone else who cannot meet the demands of standardized efficiency and productivity. The "normal" person, who has no visible defects, and who is not discriminated against for various reasons, such as ethnicity, race, nationality, class, and so on, constitutes part of the conformist framework around which "others" are discriminated. However, this is of course not an active action on the part of the "normal" people, but something that is created through the prevailing ideology. The core of the ideology is that there is something "wrong" with those who do not fit into "the norm." The "others" are thus understood as people who do not fit in, because they are "deficient" in some way, when compared to those who fulfil the demands of "the norm." In this context, it should be emphasized that a "minority body" is not an objective reality, but something that is socially constructed in relation to those who differ from a "norm." Instead of constructing an us–them relationship, between those who are within "the norm" and those with a minority body, emphasis should rather be given to the fact that diversity stimulates creativity and innovation. Discrimination by rendering people "invisible" is a matter of creating differences, so that some are within, and some are outside, the boundaries created by "the norm."

Theoretical points related to invisibility

When people are treated as "things," an experience of being overlooked arises. This experience signals that one has been made insignificant as a human being. For example, when public and commercial spaces are not freely accessible to people with disabilities, despite the fact that legislation dictates that everyone should have access. This often creates a feeling of "being a bother" due to the "difficulties" one causes. In other words, although the Disabled Persons Act was passed 50 years ago in 1970 in the United Kingdom, there are still many "no go areas" for people with disabilities (Heaton, 2014: 1).

When groups of people are subjected to a change in identity via social construction, there is a high probability that their self-image will be damaged. When you make someone "invisible" via identity change, you also confirm that the identity the person initially had was not good enough. What if this is erroneous? What if the real picture is that many of those who have a disability have a well-functioning identity, and are not interested in changing this identity? It is in such situations that the identity change is experienced as a form of coercion, i.e., one's identity is deemed not good enough, and must be changed according to the prevailing social model. This can be viewed in contrast to the affirmation model of Swain and French (2000: 569).

When you experience rejection, you are made to feel insignificant, which may be signalled by a condescending smirk. This can be experienced by the elderly, when they are subjected to ageism, i.e., being discriminated against because of one's age. In addition to ageing, many older people may also struggle with physical and emotional challenges. According to findings, people become "invisible" as they get older; not unlike the invisibility experienced by the disabled. In other words, ageism and discrimination against people with disabilities have some things in common, such as being made "invisible," and the problems encountered when attempting to enter the labour market; despite the fact that many older people are just as fully able to work as younger people, and the fact that many disabled people are also fully capable of working as non-disabled, they may experience problems in the labour market. If you use a medical model of disability, then the similarity to ageism is less. On the other hand, if you apply a social model of disability, then the similarity to ageism discrimination emerges (Oliver, 2004).

When people as a group experience rejection, the feeling may arise that an attempt is being made to change the values of the group. In its consequences, this can lead to a changed self-understanding, which can be harmful for the group and the individual members of the group. What happens in such a process is a form of alienation. We all try, disabled and others, to give our lives meaning. We become who we are through our choices, and the values we have and act on. Moreover, situations often arise when others attempt to change the meaning of our lives. It is in this process that alienation occurs. When an attempt is made to change one's values, the individual experiences a fear of losing their own value as a human being and their self-identity. When people experience alienation, their self-identity also changes.

It is claimed that society's prejudice towards people with disabilities has been greatly reduced in the last 20 years. It is possible that this applies to more active and passive discrimination techniques. However, when it comes to "invisibility," where attempts are made to change one's values, or where one experiences

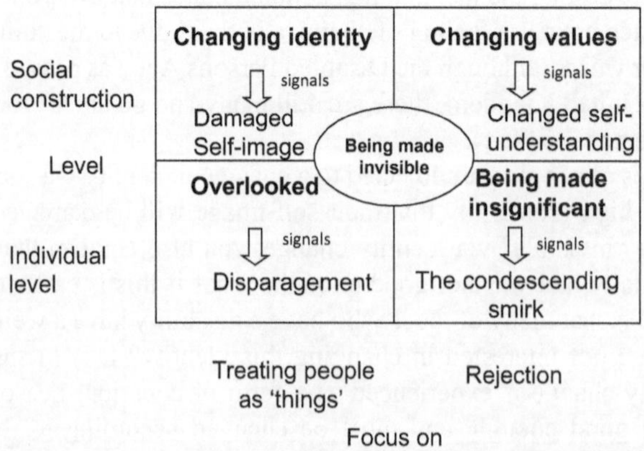

Figure 6.5 A typology of discrimination by invisibility.

being made insignificant in a social context, then it is more doubtful whether the prejudices have been particularly changed for the better. The point here is that disability is not only a question of having a minority body, but of being subjected to a socially constructed phenomenon, which consists of "a dynamic set of representations that are deeply embedded in historical and cultural contexts" (Barton, 2001: 169).

The above description is shown in a typology (Figure 6.5).

Practical utility related to invisibility

When the social barriers are not visible, it will be difficult for those who are not affected by these barriers to see what the "invisible" discrimination is about. For the disabled, on the other hand, it is a question of being prevented from full participation in social life. It seems reasonable to assume that the invisible discrimination will affect people with disabilities more strongly than active and passive discrimination. The rationale is that active and passive discrimination is easier to identify, making it possible to introduce measures against discrimination. In the case of "invisible" discrimination, it will be difficult for those who are not affected by it to understand what it concerns, precisely because it is invisible to the untrained eye.

Barriers for those with disabilities are visible everywhere. The point in this context is that it is the barriers that are not visible that are the most difficult to remove. We are not talking here about limited access to public buildings for wheelchair users. Such barriers can be removed with the help of various associations for people with disabilities and the authorities. It is precisely when barriers are invisible that the problems become difficult.

Identifying the invisible barriers for people without disabilities requires a shift in the way of thinking, or a shift in perspective; i.e., one needs to adopt the perspective of the disabled person. If this proves to be difficult in practice, then one can ask the disabled person how the invisible barriers and discrimination operate in a particular situation. To cope with this shift in perspective, it can be of great help to use Dorothy Smith's methodology of institutional ethnography (2006: 1–13; 65–89).

Goffman (1990) and Smitt (2003; 2006) point out that in order to deal with a problem that not everyone can see or understand, it is important to listen to those who experience the problem first-hand. In other words, you need to see things from the other's perspective, and put yourself in the other person's shoes in order to show empathy. Moreover, in the case of disability, you need to be aware of the fact that the problem complex is often socially constructed. Dealing with this socially constructed model is not simple, because we are culturally socialized into the medical model, where the perspective is on the individual who suffers due to his/her minority body. When you have taken the other's perspective, developed empathy with the problem and the person(s) who have experienced the problem, the next step is to accept that this is a real problem, even if you are unable to "see" the problem.

One way to tackle the "invisibility" and neglect problem is to reflect on the elements shown in Figure 6.6.

Concept		Description
Problem		The problem is identified from a specific perspective (point of view) in society and is formulated based on the point of view of the knowledge bearer.
Knowledge bearers		Those who have insight into the point of view from which the social phenomenon is examined.
Point of view		The perspective from which a social phenomenon is examined. Knowledge of the point of view is obtained through dialogue with the knowledge bearer about his/her experiences (oral or written).
Social position		The position the knowledge bearers have in society in the relevant context being investigated.
Social conditions		People's practices as it appears and is influenced by objectification.
Pervasive societal structures		Prevailing discourses or ideology.
Discourse		People participate in various discourses and reproduce them through practice, speaking, writing /preparing official documents, and so on.
Objectification		Pervasive societal structures that dominate our ideas about ourselves, and attitudes towards others and various phenomena in our environment.

Figure 6.6 Institutional ethnography: Analysis tool developed by Dagny Johannessen.

Note: This analysis tool is taken from the doctoral thesis of Dagny Johannessen, Oslo Metropolitan University, Oslo, Norway. The title of the dissertation is: "Mestringsfremmende psykososiale faktorer i overgangen fra døgnbehandling for rusavhengighet til hverdagen etterpå." (English translation: "Coping with psychosocial challenges in the transition from inpatient treatment for drug addiction to everyday life afterwards.").

Sub-conclusion related to invisibility

In this section, we examine the following question: How are people with disabilities discriminated against in the workplace by being rendered "invisible"?

The short answer is that social barriers are made invisible, so that only people with disabilities can see the barriers. When the barriers are pointed out, no one sees them but those who are affected by them every day. Attempting futilely to point out a barrier that others cannot see can affect the person's self-image and self-understanding. It can evoke a feeling of being rejected, being made small, and that you are insignificant. Making people invisible can also be related to "neglect," i.e., not understanding that there is a problem, or what the problem consists of.

Regarding neglect, which can be understood as a special variant of invisibility, one presents a problem that one feels is important, but the person one is communicating with does not understand that this can be a problem. This can also take the form of not understanding what the person experiencing the problem actually means when they explain the problem. In this way, you turn the other person into an amoeba, that has no intelligence and is impossible to communicate with. In other words, a non-entity.

On the other hand, neglect can also be understood as a negative attitude towards the person who points out the problem. This attitude can be expressed by thinking that the other person is fussing about something that is not really a problem. This is expressed in the attitude: "What's wrong now!?" The extreme of such an attitude is that it is believed that people have to manage themselves, without constantly pointing out problems, which are insignificant, made up, or do not exist.

One problem in the neglect category is when a person sitting in a wheelchair is perceived as being "retarded." Of course, this is not necessarily something that is expressed verbally, but can be shown in the tone of voice one uses when addressing a wheelchair user. People in wheelchairs can often experience being spoken to very slowly and loudly, as if they were talking to a child.

Reflection on the general research question

In this chapter, we have examined the following general research question: *How are people with disabilities discriminated against in working life?*

The short answer is that people with disabilities are discriminated against along at least three axes: Active discrimination, passive discrimination and invisibility, where a subgroup of invisibility can be called neglect.

Disability discrimination occurs in both the public and private spheres. Throughout history, certain derogatory terms have been used to describe people with disabilities. Such derogatory words tell us something about the ideology of discrimination. The historical medical term "imbecile," used by psychiatrists, to denote a certain category of people with a disability, implied how these people were undervalued in human terms; such attitudes guided the oppressive actions towards this group by medical professionals and others. If you use words and expressions with negative associations when referring to the disabled, then these people will experience that the words are real in their consequences. Discrimination against people with disabilities in working life is often linked to certain stereotypes. Stereotyping triggers pigeonholing, where people are put into categories that are imagined to be homogenous, which they seldom are. When discrimination is made into an active conceptualization, where stereotypes emerge, then various forms of discrimination will also emerge: Active and passive discrimination, and making people "invisible."

Notes

1 https://en.wikipedia.org/wiki/Bernard_of_Clairvaux
2 https://radikalportal.no/2015/07/22/det-fortiede-folkemordet-fortellingen-om-grov-historieforfalskning-og-svik/
https://en.wikipedia.org/wiki/Holocaust_victims#People_with_disabilities
3 https://en.wikipedia.org/wiki/Microaggression
4 https://en.wikipedia.org/wiki/Microaggression

References

Barton, E.I. (2001). Textual practices of erasure: Representations of disability and the founding of the United Way, in Wilson, J.C. & Lewis-Wilson, C. (eds.), *Embodied rhetorics: Disability in language and culture*, Southern Illinois University Press, Carbonsale, pp. 169–199.

Borsay, A. (2005). *Disability and social policy in Britain since 1750: A history of exclusion*, Palgrave, London.

Fougeyrollas, P. & Beauregard, L. (2001). Disability: An interactive person-environment social creation, in Albrecht, G.L.; Seelman, K.D. & Bury, M. (eds.), *Handbook of disability studies*, Sage, London, pp. 171–195.

Goffman, E. (1990). *Presentation of self in everyday life*, Penguin, New York.

Heaton, T. (2014). Access, in Cameron, C. (ed.), *Disability studies*, Sage, New York, pp. 1–3.

Heyman, J.; Ashley, S. & Moreno, G. (2014). *Disability and equity at work*, Oxford University Press, Oxford.

Kudlick, C. & Nielsen, K.E. (eds.) (2018). *The Oxford handbook of disability history*, Oxford University Press, Oxford, pp. 439–459.

Macdonald, S.J. (2015). The invisibles, in Shakespeare, T. (ed.), *Disability research today*, Routledge, London, pp. 112–132.

Mitchell, D.T. & Snyder S.L. (2015). *The biopolitics of disability*, University of Michigan Press, Ann Arbor.

Oliver, M. (1990). *The politics of disablement*, Macmillan, Basingstoke.

Oliver, M. (2004). The social model in action: If I had a hammer, in Barnes, C. & Mercer, G. (eds.), *Implementing the social model of disability: Theory and research*, The Disability Press, Leeds.Pp. 18–31.

Oliver, M. (2009). *Understanding disability*, Palgrave, London.

Patterson, L. (2018). The disability right movement in the United States, in Rembis, M.; Kudlick, C. & Nielsen, K.E. (eds.), *The Oxford Handbook of disability history*, Oxford University Press, Oxford, pp. 439–454.

Ravaud, J-F. & Stiker, H-J. (2001). Inclusion/exclusion, in Albrecht, G.L.; Seelman, K.D. & Bury, M. (eds.), *Handbook of disability studies*, Sage, London, pp. 490–515.

Read, J. (2000). *Disability, the family and society: Listening to mothers*, Open University Press, Buckingham.
Rooke, M. (2016). *Creative successful dyslexia*, Jessica Kingsley Publishers, London.
Rooke,M. (2018). *Dyslexia is my superpower (most of the time)*, Jessica Kingsley Publishers, London.
Shakespeare, T. (2015). *Disability research today*, Routledge, London.
Shakespeare, T. & Watson, N. (1997). Defending the social model, *Disability and Society*, 12(2), 293–300.
Smith, R. (2003). *Alienation and freedom*, Worldview Press, London.
Smith, D.E. (ed.). (2006). *Institutional ethnography as practice*, Roman & Littlefield, New York.
Swain, J. & French, S. (2000). *Disability on equal terms*, Sage, London.
UN. (2006). *Convention on the rights of persons with disabilities*, United Nations, New York.

Index

**Page numbers in *italics* reference figures.